SLIPCOVER
style

1

SLIPCOVER
style

ALISON
WORMLEIGHTON

NEW
BURLINGTON
BOOKS

contents

A Quarto Book

This edition published in 2003 by
New Burlington Books
The Old Brewery
6 Blundell Street
London N7 9BH

ISBN 1–86155–669–1

QUAR.SLST
Conceived, designed, and produced by
Quarto Publishing plc
The Old Brewery
6 Blundell Street
London N7 9BH

PROJECT EDITOR Fiona Robertson
ART EDITOR AND DESIGNER Sheila Volpe
ILLUSTRATOR Kate Simunek
ASSISTANT ART DIRECTOR Penny Cobb
TEXT EDITOR Anne Plume
PICTURE RESEARCH Sandra Assersohn,
    Image Select International
PROOFREADER Pamela Ellis
INDEXER Alison Wormleighton
ART DIRECTOR Moira Clinch
PUBLISHER Piers Spence

Manufactured by
Pica Digital Pte Ltd., Singapore
Printed in China
by Leefung Asco Printers Ltd.

NOTE
Throughout this book, metric equivalents
for the standard measurements are given
in parentheses. These are not exact
equivalents and are therefore not
interchangeable: use either all metric
or all standard measurements.

introduction

A SLIPCOVER IS THE PERFECT WAY to transform a faded, worn, or out-of-date chair or sofa. Not only does this removable fabric cover give an old piece of furniture a new lease on life, but it can also jazz up the whole room. Use it to inject a splash of color, reinforce your decorating theme, or add a note of comfort, luxury, coziness, or even humor—whatever effect you want. Whether you favor a sleek, tailored look or a softer, looser style, slipcovers offer an excellent opportunity to put the stamp of your own personality on your home.

Slipcovers are also supremely functional. Their original purpose, nearly four centuries ago, was to protect the more expensive, fixed upholstery underneath, and they were often removed only for formal occasions. This protective function is still one of their benefits today. If you have dining chairs upholstered in costly damask, for example, slipcovers will protect them from dust, spills, and day-to-day wear and tear. The fact that slipcovers are removable makes them highly practical and versatile. Unlike fixed upholstery, they are easy to take off to launder or dry clean. You can even have more than one cover for each piece of furniture, so that you can change them with the seasons, or when you feel like a new look.

Most chairs and sofas are suitable for slipcovering, provided they are structurally sound (you should avoid sagging springs and lumpy padding, for example) and are not upholstered in velvet or a slippery material like leather or plastic. Covers can be made for wooden chairs, too. Make sure the item is clean before you put a cover over it or the dirt will gradually work its way into the new cover.

Sewing slipcovers yourself makes them very economical. And if you want a set, for a dining room perhaps, making the second and subsequent covers is relatively quick because you can use the first as a pattern. An even greater benefit, however, is the satisfaction and pleasure you will get from having made them yourself.

Initially, the thought of making a slipcover can be daunting. Because the covers are three-dimensional, they can seem a lot more difficult than other forms of home sewing. In fact, only basic sewing skills are needed. The whole process is surprisingly straightforward and easy, with plenty of opportunity to adjust the shape and the fit before finally cutting and stitching. When the pieces of fabric are pinned together on the chair or sofa, they seem almost to mold to its contours. It is very gratifying when, with a few judicious nips and tucks, a flat piece of fabric wraps neatly and smoothly around a curved chair seat or sofa arm.

RIGHT Easy-to-make slipcovers, each in a different color, transform a set of director's chairs. To make them, see pages 66–69.

If you have not made slipcovers before, don't start with one of the more ambitious projects such as a sofa, wing chair, or set of dining chairs. The amount of pinning and stitching involved, not to mention the cost of the fabric, can be overwhelming at first. A simple slipcover like the short tailored cover on pages 70–73 is ideal, as it is quick and easy but will still acquaint you with the basic techniques. Before you tackle any projects, however, be sure to read the Techniques section at the back of the book (pages 98–125).

The projects include most of the classic styles of slipcovers and the main types of chairs and sofas, as well as some fun, unusual designs. There are also projects for making covers for furniture other than conventional chairs and sofas, such as deck chairs, beds, and tables.

Even when projects look very different, similar techniques are used, and once you become familiar with these, you will be able to create your own designs. This is because slipcovers are combinations of many interchangeable aspects. If you like the skirt on one but have to have the arms of another, it probably won't be difficult to put them together. That's one of the most rewarding aspects of making slipcovers—you can create your own concoctions to suit your own particular needs.

EQUIPMENT

You don't need much equipment to make slipcovers, but you do need a sewing machine. A basic model is perfectly adequate. (If you do a lot of sewing, you may already be using an overlock machine, or serger, on which you can stitch, finish, and trim seams all in one step.) Always follow the directions in the manual when using the machine.

To measure curved surfaces, you'll need a synthetic or fiberglass flexible 60 inch (150cm) tape measure. To measure flat or gently curved surfaces, use a retractable steel tape measure. A long straightedge such as a yardstick is best for marking long, straight edges. For checking that corners are square, a carpenter's square is useful, but you could improvise with a large book.

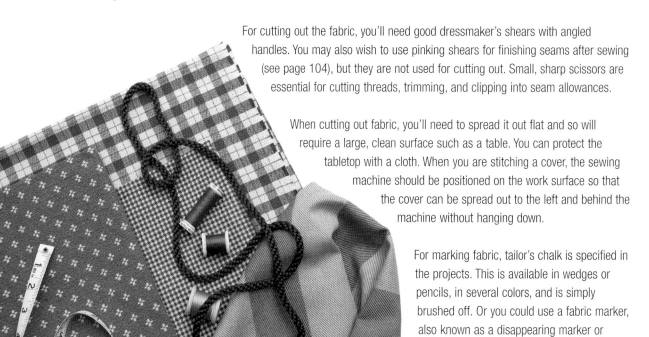

For cutting out the fabric, you'll need good dressmaker's shears with angled handles. You may also wish to use pinking shears for finishing seams after sewing (see page 104), but they are not used for cutting out. Small, sharp scissors are essential for cutting threads, trimming, and clipping into seam allowances.

When cutting out fabric, you'll need to spread it out flat and so will require a large, clean surface such as a table. You can protect the tabletop with a cloth. When you are stitching a cover, the sewing machine should be positioned on the work surface so that the cover can be spread out to the left and behind the machine without hanging down.

For marking fabric, tailor's chalk is specified in the projects. This is available in wedges or pencils, in several colors, and is simply brushed off. Or you could use a fabric marker, also known as a disappearing marker or vanishing pen—some types fade away within about two days, while others can be removed with water. Don't use the latter on fabric that will show watermarks. Test the marker on scrap fabric before using it, to make sure the marks really do disappear. Also, avoid ironing over the marks before they have been removed, as this may permanently set them.

When pinning seams, ordinary dressmaker's pins can be used, but long pins with colored glass or plastic heads are much easier to see and to handle. To anchor fabric pieces to the upholstery when pin-fitting (see page 102), T-pins are best. These are long, sturdy pins shaped like the letter T. If you can't find them, glass-headed pins can be used. Use the latter when pin-fitting on non-upholstered chairs and sofas.

You will also need hand-sewing needles. Use those known as "sharps" for general hand sewing, and those known as "milliner's needles" for long hand-basting or gathering stitches. The only other essential equipment is a steam iron for pressing fabric. Use it with a "press cloth," such as a man's handkerchief or a piece of muslin. Optional extra items that will come in handy are chalk for marking the centers of wooden or wicker chairs; a pin cushion or a magnetic pin caddy; twist pins, which have plastic heads and twisted stems, for holding slipcovers in place out of sight; and a seam ripper, for ripping out seams quickly.

MATERIALS

The materials you will need are specified at the beginning of each project. The principal item, obviously, is fabric, so be sure to read page 99 before buying any fabric for a project. An all-purpose polyester thread can be used for both natural and synthetic fabrics, or you could use cotton thread for cotton and linen fabrics, and polyester thread for synthetics. The thread should be the same color as the fabric, but if necessary go for one marginally darker rather than lighter.

Other materials used in many of the projects include purchased bias binding (though making your own is preferable and sometimes essential), piping cord, upholstery zippers, and hook-and-loop tape such as Velcro (see pages 116, 120, 112, and 113 respectively). Large sheets of paper are used for making templates, and graph paper can be used if you wish for scale drawings of cutting layouts. Polyester batting, which is washable, is often used for padding; it comes in sheets of various weights, and is also available loose as fiberfill.

Once you have your basic sewing kit, all that remains is to get out your shears and your pin cushion, choose a project, find a fabric you love—and make a start!

PLEATED COVER FOR WING CHAIR

DEEP, CRISP PLEATS AT THE CORNERS OF THE SKIRT AND AN UNFUSSY DESIGN MAKE THIS SNUG-FITTING, TAILORED SLIPCOVER IDEAL FOR A CLASSIC WING CHAIR.

MATERIALS

Decorator fabric

Matching thread

¼ in (5mm) thick piping cord

Upholstery zipper

TECHNIQUES

Pin-fitting (page 102)

Tuck-ins (page 114)

Shaping (page 108)

Corners (page 106)

Piping (page 120)

Zippers (page 112)

Inverted pleats (page 108)

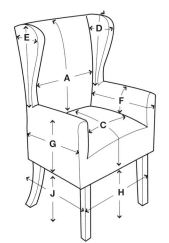

MEASURING

Measure each section at the widest points, as the cover will be cut as a series of rectangles. The zipper should be 2 in (5cm) shorter than the distance from the floor to the top of the chair back at the side.

● This cover is designed for a wing chair with straight arms but could be adapted for scroll arms (see page 15).

Inside back (A): *width:* width of inside back between wings, plus 16 in (40.5cm); *length:* distance from top rear edge of back, over top of back, and down to seat, plus 10 in (25.5cm).

Outside back (B): *width:* width of outside back, plus 4 in (10cm); *length:* distance from top of back to bottom of seat, plus 4 in (10cm).

Seat (C): *width:* width of seat between arms, plus 16 in (40.5cm); *length:* distance from inside back to front, and then down to bottom of seat, plus 10 in (25.5cm).

Inside wing (D): *width:* distance from outer edge of front of wing, across front of wing, to inside back,

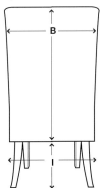

plus 10 in (25.5cm); *length:* distance from top of wing at outside edge, across top of wing, and down to arm, plus 10 in (25.5cm).

Outside wing (E): *width:* distance from front of wing to outside back, plus 4 in (10cm); *length:* distance from top of wing to arm, plus 4 in (10cm).

Inside arm (F): *width:* distance from outer edge of front of arm, across front of arm, to inside back, plus 10 in (25.5cm); *length:* distance from top of arm at outside, across top of arm, and down to seat, plus 10 in (25.5cm).

Outside arm (G): *width:* distance from front of arm to outside back, plus 4 in (10cm); *length:* distance from top of arm to bottom of seat at outside, plus 4 in (10cm).

Skirt front (H): *width:* width of chair at bottom of seat, plus 14 in (35.5cm); *length:* distance from bottom of seat to floor, plus 3 in (7.5cm).

Skirt back (I): *width:* width of chair at bottom of seat, plus 2 in (5cm); *length:* distance from bottom of seat to floor, plus 3 in (7.5cm).

Skirt side (J): *width:* distance from front to back at bottom of seat, plus 8 in (20.5cm); *length:* distance from bottom of seat to floor, plus 3 in (7.5cm).

Bias strip (K): *width:* 2 in (5cm); *length:* distance around seat, plus 10 in (25.5cm), plus distance from bottom of seat at front, up arm and wing, across top of back, and down other wing and arm to bottom of seat.

TYPICAL YARDAGES

To cover a chair 30 in (76cm) wide and 39 in (1m) high, using fabric 54 in (137cm) wide, you would need about 6½ yd (6m) of fabric, plus 10 x the pattern repeat. To match the pattern crosswise too, or to use fabric 45 in (115cm) wide, would require about 10 yd (9.2m), plus 15 x the lengthwise pattern repeat.

CUTTING OUT

Cut 1 x A, 1 x B, 1 x C, 2 x D, 2 x E, 2 x F, 2 x G, 1 x H, 1 x I, and 2 x J, making sure the pattern (or the nap, if there is one) runs from top to bottom or from back to front. Also make sure the pattern of each piece will match that of each adjacent piece. Mark the letters on the pieces.

From the same fabric (or contrasting fabric, if you prefer), cut out and join bias strips as necessary, to produce 1 x K for piping the seams.

IMPORTANT: Because this cover is snug, all fabric pieces should be placed on the chair right side up; initially, seams are pinned with wrong sides together (then in step 9 repinned with right sides together). A seam allowance should be trimmed to 1 in (2.5cm) once you have pinned together the pieces for that seam; it will be trimmed to its final ⅝ in (1.5cm) later.

1 Make enough piping to pipe the chair at the top (arms, wings, and back) and above the skirt. Use pins to mark the height of the skirt all the way around the chair, measuring from the floor up. Also use pins to mark the centers of the chair inside back, outside back, and seat, and of the inside back (A), outside back (B), and seat (C) fabric pieces.

2 Place the inside back (A) on the chair, lining up the center with that of the chair. Matching centers, pin the outside back (B) to the inside back (A) across the top; trim. Smooth the inside back (A) over the chair and anchor it with T-pins. Do the same for the outside back (B).

3 Position the seat (C) on the chair. Matching centers, pin the seat (C) to the inside back (A), creating a tuck-in of 3–6 in (7.5–15cm); trim. Smooth the fabric over the chair seat and onto the front of the chair, anchoring it with T-pins.

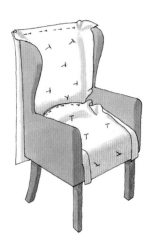

TYPICAL CUTTING LAYOUT FOR 54 IN (137CM) WIDE FABRIC

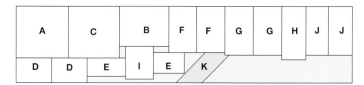

A		C		B	F	F	G	G	H	J	J
D	D	E		I	E	K					

4 Position the inside arm (F) on the chair. Anchor the fabric along the top, smooth it down over the arm, and anchor it near the bottom of the arm with T-pins. Pin it to the seat (C) and also to the inside back (A), creating tuck-ins of 3–6 in (7.5–15cm) at both; trim. Clip into the seam allowance of the inside arm (F) where the inside back (A) meets the seat (C). Make small pleats or darts on the outer edge to curve the fabric over the front of the arm. Repeat for the opposite side.

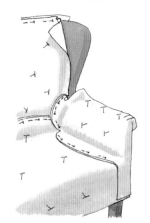

5 Anchor the outside arm (G) to the chair arm and side with T-pins, smoothing it into place and checking that the grain is at right angles to the floor. Pin the outside arm (G) to the inside arm (F) along the outer top edge of the chair arm, and to the outside back (B); trim. Repeat for the opposite side. Trim the lower edge of both outside arms (G), the outside back (B), and the seat (C) 1 in (2.5cm) below the pins marking the skirt height.

6 Anchor the inside wing (D) to the inside wing of the chair with T-pins. Pin it to the inside back (A), creating a tuck-in of 3–6 in (7.5–15cm); trim. Make small pleats or darts on the outer edge to fit the curve of the wing. Pin the lower edge of the inside wing (D) to the back edge of the inside arm (F), clipping into the seam allowance of the latter where it meets the inside back (A); trim. Repeat for the opposite side.

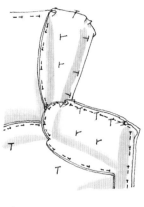

7 Anchor the outside wing (E) to the outside wing of the chair with T-pins. Pin it to the outside back (B) and the outside arm (G); trim. Now pin it to the inside wing (D) along the outer edge of the chair wing; trim, clipping into the seam allowance on the curve. Also clip into the seam allowance of the outside arm (G) at the point where it meets the outside wing (E) and the inside arm (F). Repeat for the opposite side.

8 Using tailor's chalk, mark each seamline on the wrong side. Remove the T-pins anchoring the fabric to the chair. Unpin the seam at the outside back right of the chair, apart from the top 2 in (5cm), and remove the cover. Using a straightedge, redraw any lines that are not straight (without making the cover smaller). Trim all the seam allowances to ⅝ in (1.5cm) except for the one at back right, which should remain 1 in (2.5cm).

9 Unpin one portion of the cover at a time, and repin the pieces with right sides together before moving on to unpin and repin the next section. As you do so, insert a single length of piping into the seams between the inside arm (F) and outside arm (G); inside wing (D) and outside wing (E); and inside back (A) and outside back (B). Check the fit on the chair, pushing in the tuck-ins. Trim the lower edge so that it is ⅝ in (1.5cm) beneath the height of the skirt.

10 Stitch the seams, leaving ⅝ in (1.5cm) unstitched at the ends, and pivoting at corners or stitching into them. Stitch the piped seams as one continuous seam, after stitching the other seams that meet it. Stitch only the top 2 in (5cm) of the back right-hand seam, as the zipper will be applied here (see step 13). Finish the raw edges of the stitched seams and press them open. Baste piping along the lower edge of the cover on the right side, allowing for a ⅝ in (1.5cm) seam; clip into the piping seam allowance at the corners.

11 With right sides together, stitch the two skirt sides (J) to the skirt front (H) along the side edges with 1 in (2.5cm) seams, leaving ⅝ in (1.5cm) unstitched at the top. Stitch the skirt back (I) to the left side in the same way. Trim the stitched seam allowances to ⅝ in (1.5cm), finish the seams, and press them open. Put the cover back on the chair, wrong side out.

12 With right sides together, pin the top edge of the skirt to the lower edge of the cover, lining up the seams with the chair corners. Form the excess fabric into an inverted pleat at each front corner, with the seam at the center. Remove the cover. Baste along the length of the pleats; press, then remove the basting. Stitch the skirt to the cover with a ⅝ in (1.5cm) seam; finish the seam, and press. Put the cover on the chair right side out, and pin the unstitched seam closed temporarily.

13 Press under a double 1 in (2.5cm) hem at the lower edge, trimming off excess fabric first; hand sew the hem. Unpin the unstitched seam, remove the cover, and install the zipper. Put the cover back on the chair, close the zipper, and push in the tuck-ins.

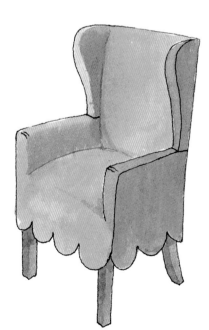

VARIATION

Omit the skirt, make the rest of the cover a little longer, and add a scalloped lower edge. To make scallops, see pages 76–77 (Bedcover, steps 3–4).

PLEATED SCROLL-ARM SOFA COVER

A TIGHT-FITTING SLIPCOVER FOR A TRADITIONAL SCROLL-ARM SOFA WITH BOX CUSHIONS GIVES YOU THE BEST OF BOTH WORLDS—A SMART LOOK PLUS EASY CLEANING. THE SAME TECHNIQUES ARE USED FOR AN ARMCHAIR IN THIS STYLE.

MATERIALS

Decorator fabric

Matching thread

¼ in (5mm) thick piping cord

2 upholstery zippers for sofa cover and
one for each cushion

TECHNIQUES

Pin-fitting (page 102)

Tuck-ins (page 114)

Shaping (page 108)

Corners (page 106)

Piping (page 120)

Zippers (page 112)

Inverted pleats (page 108)

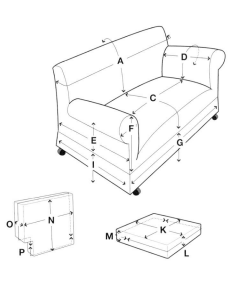

MEASURING

Remove the cushions before measuring the sofa.
Measure each section at the widest points, as the
cover will be cut as a series of rectangles. Each sofa
zipper should each be 2 in (5cm) shorter than the
height of the sofa back at the side, from top to floor.
Each cushion zipper should be 4 in (10cm) longer
than the back edge of the cushion.

 • This cover is designed for a sofa or chair with
scroll arms but could be adapted for straight arms
(see page 11). Here the arm seam is underneath
the scroll, but, depending on the sofa or chair
design, it could be placed halfway around the
scroll instead.

Inside back (A): *width:* distance from one side
edge of outside back, across inside back to other
side edge of outside back, plus 4 in (10cm); *length:*
distance from top edge of outside back, over top of
back, and down to seat, plus 10 in (25.5cm).

Outside back (B): *width:* width of outside back,
plus 4 in (10cm); *length:* distance from top of back
to bottom of seat, plus 4 in (10cm).

Seat (C): *width:* width of seat, plus 16 in (40.5cm);
length: distance from inside back to front and then
down to bottom of seat, plus 10 in (25.5cm).

Inside arm (D): *width:* distance from front of arm to
inside back, plus 11 in (28cm); *length:* distance
from beneath scroll at outside, over top of arm, and
down to seat, plus 11 in (28cm)).

Outside arm (E): *width:* distance from front of arm
to outside back, plus 5 in (13cm); *length:* distance
from beneath scroll at outside, to bottom of seat,
plus 5 in (13cm).

Front arm (F): *width:* width of front of arm plus 4 in
(10cm); *length:* distance from top of arm to bottom
of seat, plus 4 in (10cm).

Skirt front (G): *width:* width of sofa at bottom of
seat, plus 14 in (35.5cm); *length:* distance from
bottom of seat to floor, plus 3 in (7.5cm).

Skirt back (H): *width:* width of sofa at bottom of
seat, plus 2½ in (6.5cm); *length:* distance from
bottom of seat to floor, plus 3 in (7.5cm).

Skirt side (I): *width:* distance from front to back
at bottom of seat, plus 8 in (20.5cm); *length:*
distance from bottom of seat to floor, plus
3 in (7.5cm).

Bias strip (J): *width:* 2 in (5cm); *length:* about
15½ yd (14m) for a three-seater sofa.

Seat cushion top/bottom (K): *width:* width of
cushion, plus 4 in (10cm); *length:* distance from
front to back of cushion, plus 4 in (10cm).

Seat cushion boxing strip (L): *width:* thickness
of cushion, plus 1¼ in (3cm); *length:* distance
around cushion, less width of cushion at back,
less 3½ in (9cm).

Seat cushion zipper strip (M): *width:* ½ thickness
of cushion, plus 1⅝ in (4cm); *length:* width of
cushion at back, plus 6 in (15cm).

TYPICAL CUTTING LAYOUT FOR 54 IN (137CM) WIDE FABRIC

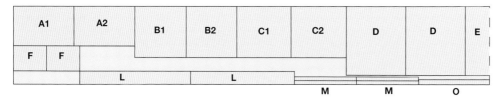

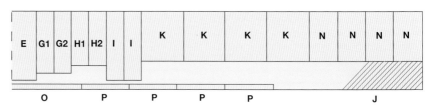

Back cushion top/bottom (N):

width: width of cushion at top, plus 4 in (10cm); *length:* distance from top to bottom of cushion, plus 4 in (10cm).

Back cushion boxing strip (O):

width: thickness of cushion, plus 1¼ in (3cm); *length:* distance around cushion, less width of cushion at bottom, less 3½ in (9cm).

Back cushion zipper strip (P):
width: ½ thickness of cushion, plus 1⅝ in (4cm); *length:* width of cushion at bottom, plus 6 in (15cm).

TYPICAL YARDAGES

To cover a sofa 67 in (170cm) wide, using fabric 54 in (137cm) wide, you would need about 18¼ yd (17m) of fabric, excluding the pattern repeat.

CUTTING OUT

Cut 1 x A, 1 x B, 1 x C, 2 x D, 2 x E, 2 x F, 1 x G, 1 x H, and 2 x I. For each seat cushion cut 2 x K, 1 x L, and 2 x M, and for each back cushion cut 2 x N, 1 x O, and 2 x P. Make sure the pattern (or the nap, if there is one) runs from top to bottom or from back to front. Also make sure the pattern of each piece will match that of each adjacent piece. Mark the letters on the pieces. You will have to join widths for the inside back (A), outside back (B), seat (C), skirt front (G), and skirt back (H), with the seams matching.

From the same fabric (or contrasting fabric, if you prefer), cut out and join bias strips as necessary, to produce 1 x J for piping the seams.

IMPORTANT: Because this cover is snug, all fabric pieces should be placed on the sofa right side up; initially, seams are pinned with wrong sides together (then in step 8 repinned with right sides together). A seam allowance should be trimmed to 1 in (2.5cm) once you have pinned together the pieces for that seam; it will be trimmed to its final ⅝ in (1.5cm) later.

1 Make enough piping to pipe the seams. Join fabric pieces to make the wide pieces (see Cutting Out). Use pins to mark the height of the skirt all the way around the sofa, measuring from the floor up. Also use pins to mark the centers of the sofa inside back, outside back, and seat, and of the inside back (A), outside back (B), and seat (C) fabric pieces.

2 Place the inside back (A) on the sofa, lining up the center with that of the sofa. Matching centers, pin the outside back (B) to the inside back (A) across the top. Smooth the inside back (A) over the sofa back, and anchor it with T-pins. Do the same for the outside back. Pin the two pieces down the sides of the sofa outside back. Trim. Make darts in the inside back (A) at the corners.

3 Position the seat (C) on the sofa. Matching centers, pin the seat (C) to the inside back (A), creating a tuck-in of 3–6 in (7.5–15cm); trim. Smooth the fabric over the sofa seat and down onto the front, anchoring it with T-pins.

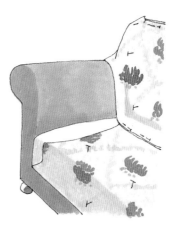

4 Position the inside arm (D) on the sofa. Anchor the fabric along the top, smooth it down over the arm, and anchor it near the bottom of the arm with T-pins. Pin it to the seat (C) and to the inside back (A), creating tuck-ins of 3–6 in (7.5–15cm) at both; trim. Clip into the seam allowance of the inside arm (D) where the inside back (A) meets the seat (C). Make small pleats or darts on the outer edge of the inside arm (D) to curve it over the front of the arm. Repeat for the opposite side.

5 Anchor the outside arm (E) to the sofa arm and side with T-pins, smoothing it into place and checking that the grain is at right angles to the floor. Pin it to the inside arm (D), to the inside back (A), and to the outside back (B); trim, clipping into the seam allowances on the curves. Repeat for the opposite side.

9 Stitch the seams, leaving ⅝ in (1.5cm) unstitched at the ends, and pivoting at corners or stitching into them. Stitch only the top 2 in (5cm) of the two back, vertical seams. Check the fit, then finish the raw edges of the stitched seams; press them open. Clip into seam allowances on curves. Baste piping along the lower edge of the cover on the right side, allowing for a ⅝ in (1.5cm) seam; clip into the seam allowance at the corners.

10 With right sides together, stitch the two skirt sides (I) to the skirt front (G) along the side edges with ⅝ in (1.5cm) seams, leaving ⅝ in (1.5cm) unstitched at the top. Trim the stitched seam allowances to ⅝ in (1.5cm), finish the seams, and press them open.

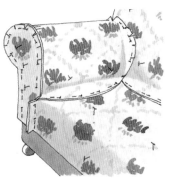

6 With T-pins, anchor the front arm (F) to the front of the sofa arm. Pin it to the inside arm (D) and outside arm (E). Trim, clipping into the seam allowance on the curves. Pin it to the front (vertical) part of the seat (C), clipping into the seam allowance of the seat (C) at the front corner; trim. Repeat for the opposite side.

7 Using tailor's chalk, mark each seamline on the wrong side. Remove the T-pins anchoring the fabric to the sofa. Unpin the seams at the back of the sofa, apart from the top 2 in (5cm), and remove the cover. Trim all the seam allowances to ⅝ in (1.5cm) except for the two back ones, which should remain 1 in (2.5cm).

8 Unpin one portion of the cover at a time, and repin the pieces with right sides together before moving on to unpin and repin the next section. As you do so, insert piping into the seams. Check the fit on the sofa, pushing in the tuck-ins. Trim the lower edge so that it is ⅝ in (1.5cm) beneath the height of the skirt.

11 With right sides together, pin the skirt back (H) to the cover. Pin the skirt front/sides (G/I) to the rest of the cover, lining up seams with corners. Form the excess fabric at each front corner into an inverted pleat with the seam at the center. Baste and press the pleats, then remove the basting. Stitch the skirt to the cover with ⅝ in (1.5cm) seams; finish seams and press. Put the cover back on the sofa. Pin the unstitched back seams closed temporarily.

12 Press under a double 1 in (2.5cm) hem at the lower edge, trimming off excess fabric first; hand sew the hem. Unpin the unstitched seams, remove the cover, and install a zipper in each. Put the cover back on the sofa, close the zippers, and push in the tuck-ins.

13 Make up the back and seat cushions as for the cushions on pages 21 (steps 14–17) and 51 (step 10), inserting piping in the seams.

TIE-BACK WING CHAIR COVER WITH T-CUSHION

THIS LOOSE-FITTING SLIPCOVER, WHICH HAS UNSTITCHED BACK SEAMS HELD TOGETHER WITH TIES, MAKES ANY WING CHAIR LOOK COMFY AND INVITING, PARTICULARLY WITH THE DEEP, SQUASHY T-CUSHION.

MATERIALS
Decorator fabric
Matching thread
Upholstery zipper
for cushion

TECHNIQUES
Pin-fitting (page 102)
Corners (page 106)
Shaping (page 108)
Zippers (page 112)

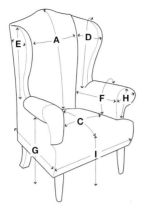

MEASURING
Remove the cushion before measuring the
chair. Measure each section at the widest points, as the cover
will be cut as a series of rectangles. The zipper should be 4 in
(10cm) longer than the back edge of the cushion.

● The cover is designed for a wing chair with scroll arms but
could be adapted for straight arms (see page 11). Here the arm
seam is halfway around the scroll, but, depending on the chair design, it
could be placed beneath the scroll instead. Here, the Queen Anne-style
seat projects beyond the arms at the front, but the cover design could be
adapted (see pages 14–17).

Inside back (A): *width:* width of inside back between wings, plus 17 in (43cm);
length: distance from top back edge of back, over top of back, and down to seat,
plus 11 in (28cm).

Outside back (B): *width:* width of outside back, plus 5 in (13cm); *length:* distance
from top of back to floor, plus 5 in (13cm).

Seat (C): *width:* width of seat between arms, plus 17 in (43cm); *length:* distance
from inside back to front of arms, plus 11 in (28cm).

Inside wing (D): *width:* distance from outer edge of front of wing, across front of
wing, to inside back, plus 11 in (28cm); *length:* distance from top of wing at outside
edge, across top of wing, and down to arm, plus 11 in (28cm).

Outside wing (E): *width:* distance from front of wing to outside back, plus 5 in
(13cm); *length:* distance from top of wing to arm, plus 5 in (13cm).

Inside arm (F): *width:* distance from front of arm to inside back, plus 11 in (28cm);
length: distance from halfway around scroll at outside, across top of arm, and down
to seat, plus 11 in (28cm).

Outside arm (G): *width:* distance from front of seat to outside back, plus 5 in (13cm);
length: distance from halfway around scroll at outside, to floor, plus 5 in (13cm).

Front arm (H): *width:* width of front of arm plus
4 in (10cm); *length:* distance from top of arm to
top of seat, plus 5 in (13cm).

Front (I): *width:* width of front at seat
level, plus 5 in (13cm); *length:* distance
from front of arm over seat and down to
floor, plus 5 in (13cm).

Ties (J): *width:* 4 in (10cm);
length: 18 in (45.5cm).

Cushion top/bottom (K): *width:*
width of cushion at wide "T-bar,"
plus 4 in (10cm); *length:* distance
from front to back of cushion, plus
4 in (10cm).

Cushion boxing strip (L): *width:*
thickness of cushion, plus 1¼ in
(3cm); *length:* distance around
cushion, less width of cushion at back,
less 3½ in (9cm).

Cushion zipper strip (M): *width:*
½ thickness of cushion, plus 1⅝ in
(4cm); *length:* width of cushion at back, plus
6 in (15cm).

TYPICAL YARDAGES
To cover a chair 30 in (76cm) wide and 39 in (1m)
high, using fabric 54 in (137cm) wide, you would
need about 7¼ yd (6.6m) of fabric, plus 8 x the
pattern repeat. To match the pattern crosswise too,
or to use fabric 45 in (115cm) wide, would require
about twice that amount.

CUTTING OUT
Cut 1 x A, 1 x B, 1 x C, 2 x D, 2 x E, 2 x F, 2 x G,
2 x H, 1 x I, 12 x J, 2 x K, 1 x L, and 2 x M, making
sure the pattern (or the nap, if there is one) runs
from top to bottom or from back to front. However,
the inside arm (F) can be cut on the crosswise grain
if you wish, as in the photograph, and so can the
ties (J). Also make sure the pattern of each piece
will match that of each adjacent piece. Mark the
letters on the pieces.

IMPORTANT: Because this cover is quite loose, all
fabric pieces can be placed on the chair wrong side
up; seams are pinned with right sides together. A
seam allowance should be trimmed to 1 in (2.5cm)
once you have pinned together the pieces for that
seam; it will be trimmed to its final ⅝ in (1.5cm) later.

TYPICAL CUTTING LAYOUT FOR 54 IN (137CM) WIDE FABRIC
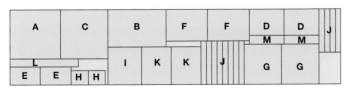

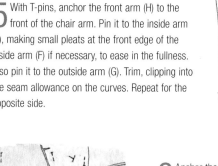

5 With T-pins, anchor the front arm (H) to the front of the chair arm. Pin it to the inside arm (F), making small pleats at the front edge of the inside arm (F) if necessary, to ease in the fullness. Also pin it to the outside arm (G). Trim, clipping into the seam allowance on the curves. Repeat for the opposite side.

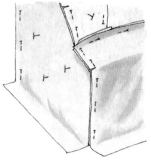

6 Anchor the front (I) to the chair with T-pins. Pin the top edge to the seat (C) and to the front arm (H). Also pin the side edge to the top and side of the outside arm (G), clipping into the seam allowance of the front (I) at the front corner of the chair; trim. Repeat for the opposite side.

1 Use pins to mark the centers of the chair inside back, outside back, and seat, and of the inside back (A), outside back (B), and seat (C) fabric pieces. Place the inside back (A) on the chair, lining up the center with that of the chair. Matching centers, pin the outside back (B) to the inside back (A) across the top; trim. Smooth the inside back (A) over the chair and anchor it with T-pins. Do the same for the outside back (B).

2 Position the seat (C) on the chair. Matching centers, pin the seat (C) to the inside back (A), creating a tuck-in of 3–6 in (7.5–15cm); trim. Smooth the fabric over the chair seat and the front, anchoring it with T-pins.

7 Anchor the inside wing (D) to the inside wing of the chair with T-pins. Pin it to the inside back (A), creating a tuck-in of 3–6 in (7.5–15cm); trim. Make small pleats or darts on the outer edge to fit the curve of the wing. Pin the lower edge of the inside wing (D) to the back edge of the inside arm (F), clipping into the seam allowance of the latter where it meets the inside back (A); trim. Repeat for the opposite side.

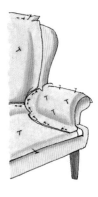

3 Position the inside arm (F) on the chair arm. Anchor the fabric along the top with T-pins, smooth it down over the arm, and anchor it near the bottom of the arm with more T-pins. Pin it to the seat (C) and also to the inside back (A), creating tuck-ins of 3–6 in (7.5–15cm) at both; trim. Clip into the seam allowance of the inside arm (F) where the inside back (A) meets the seat (C). Repeat for the opposite side.

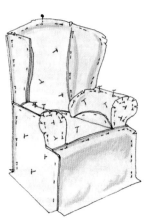

8 Anchor the outside wing (E) to the outside wing of the chair with T-pins. Pin it to the outside back (B) and the outside arm (G); trim. Now pin it to the inside wing (D) along the outer edge of the chair wing; trim, clipping into the seam allowance on the curve. Also clip into the seam allowance of the outside arm (G) at the point where it meets the outside wing (E) and the inside arm (F). Repeat for the opposite side.

4 Anchor the outside arm (G) to the chair arm and side with T-pins, smoothing it into place and checking that the grain is at right angles to the floor. Pin it to the inside arm (F) and to the outside back (B); trim, clipping into the seam allowances on the curves. Repeat for the opposite side.

9 Using tailor's chalk, mark each seamline. Remove the T-pins anchoring the fabric to the chair, and remove the cover from the chair. Using a straightedge, redraw any lines that are not straight. Trim all the seam allowances to ⅝ in (1.5cm), except for the two vertical back ones, which should remain 1 in (2.5cm).

10 Check the fit on the chair. Stitch all the seams except the vertical back ones, leaving ⅝ in (1.5cm) unstitched at the ends (except on the lower edge), and pivoting at corners or stitching into them.

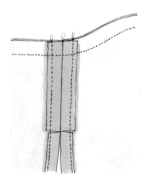

11 Stitch only the top 6 in (15cm) of each vertical back seam. Clip into the seam allowances at the end of the stitching, and press open the stitched portion of each seam. Press under ¼ in (5mm) and then ¾ in (2cm) on the seam allowances of the unstitched portion. Stitch in place, continuing the stitching onto the stitched portion.

12 Press under a double 1 in (2.5cm) hem at the lower edge, trimming off excess fabric first; hand sew the hem.

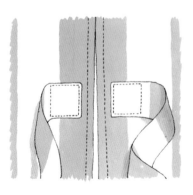

13 For the ties, fold each of the fabric pieces (J) in half lengthwise, with right sides together; pin and stitch a ⅜ in (1cm) seam down the long edge and across one end. Turn the ties right side out; press. Turn in the raw edges at the end, and slipstitch. Attach three pairs of ties on either side of each opening, as shown, spacing them equally.

14 Unlike other box cushions, covers for T-cushions should be pin-fitted. With T-pins, anchor the top (K), wrong side up, to the cushion along the seamlines, smoothing out the fabric. With a fabric marker or tailor's chalk, mark the seamlines, then remove the T-pins. Straighten the lines using a straightedge, and adjust slightly if the piece is not symmetrical. Trim the seam allowances to ⅝ in (1.5cm). Use this piece as a template to cut out the back from the other piece (K).

15 With right sides together, pin the two zipper strips (M) together along one long edge. Stitch a 1 in (2.5cm) seam for 1 in (2.5cm) at each end, machine basting in between. Install the zipper, then remove the basting and open the zipper.

16 With right sides together, stitch the ends of the boxing strip (L) to those of the zipper section with ⅝ in (1.5cm) seams. Check the fit by slipping the strip onto the cushion; the zipper goes at the back, extending equally around each corner. The strip should fit closely around the cushion. At the corners, clip into the seam allowances. Remove the strip and press the seams open.

17 With right sides together, pin and then stitch the strip to the top and bottom pieces (K) with ⅝ in (1.5cm) seams. Trim the seams and corners, turn the cover right side out, and press. Insert the cushion and close the zipper.

VARIATION

Instead of using ties at the back of the chair cover, insert grommets down the sides of the two seams, and lace the openings closed with cords. Finish halfway down, tying each pair of cords in a bow.

COVER FOR BOX-STYLE SOFA

DESIGNED FOR THE CLASSIC BOX-STYLE SOFA (OR CHAIR) WITH CLUB
ARMS, A SLEEK COVER LIKE THIS LOOKS LIKE FITTED UPHOLSTERY.

MATERIALS

Decorator fabric
Matching thread
Sew-and-stick Velcro
2 upholstery zippers

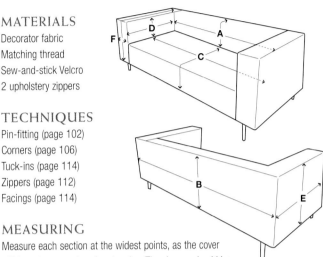

TECHNIQUES

Pin-fitting (page 102)
Corners (page 106)
Tuck-ins (page 114)
Zippers (page 112)
Facings (page 114)

MEASURING

Measure each section at the widest points, as the cover
will be cut as a series of rectangles. The zippers should be
2 in (5cm) shorter than the distance from the top of the back to the
lower edge.

• The cover is designed for a sofa that doesn't have a boxing strip between the
inside back and outside back. If your sofa does have one, you will need to make a
boxing strip with dimensions the same as those of the sofa boxing strip, plus 4 in
(10cm) each way, joining widths as necessary (see Cutting Out). The inside back (A)
will then be measured only from the top of the sofa inside back. The boxing strip is
pin-fitted and pinned to the inside back (A) and outside back (B) in step 2.

Inside back (A): *width:* width of inside back, plus 16 in (40.5cm); *length:*
distance from top edge of outside back, over top of back, and down to seat, plus
10 in (25.5cm).

Outside back (B): *width:* width of outside back (to outer edges), plus 4 in (10cm);
length: distance from top of back to lower edge, plus 4 in (10cm).

Seat (C): *width:* width of seat, plus 16 in (40.5cm); *length:* distance from inside
back to front and then down to lower edge, plus 10 in (25.5cm).

Inside arm (D): *width:* distance from front of arm to inside back, plus 10 in
(25.5cm); *length:* distance from top of arm to seat, plus 10 in (25.5cm).

Outside arm (E): *width:* distance from front of arm to outside back, plus 4 in
(10cm); *length:* distance from top of arm to lower edge, plus 4 in (10cm).

Side boxing strip (F): *width:* width of top of arm, plus 4 in (10cm); *length:* distance
from outside back to front of arm, and then down to lower edge, plus 4 in (10cm).

TYPICAL YARDAGES

To cover a sofa 72 in (183cm) wide and 27 in (69cm) high, using fabric 54 in
(137cm) wide, you need about 8½ yd (8m) of fabric, excluding the pattern repeat.

TYPICAL CUTTING LAYOUT FOR 54 IN (137CM) WIDE FABRIC

A1	B1	C1	A3	B3		F		F	
A2	B2	C2		C3	D	D	E		E

CUTTING OUT

Cut 1 x A, 1 x B, 1 x C, 2 x D, 2 x E, and 2 x F, making sure the pattern (or the nap, if there is one) runs from top to bottom or from back to front. Also make sure the pattern of each piece will match that of each adjacent piece. Mark the letters on the pieces. Unless you cut the fabric so that the lengthwise grain runs along the length of the sofa, you will have to join widths for the inside back (A), outside back (B), and seat (C), with the seams matching.

IMPORTANT: Because this cover is snug, all fabric pieces should be placed on the sofa right side up; initially, seams are pinned with wrong sides together (then in step 10 repinned with right sides together). A seam allowance should be trimmed to 1 in (2.5cm) once you have pinned together the pieces for that seam; it will be trimmed to its final ⅝ in (1.5cm) later.

1 Join fabric pieces to make the wide pieces (see Cutting Out). Use pins to mark the centers of the sofa inside back, outside back, and seat, and of the inside back (A), outside back (B), and seat (C) fabric pieces.

2 Place the inside back (A) on the sofa, lining up the center with that of the sofa. Matching centers, pin the outside back (B) to the inside back (A) across the top; trim. Smooth the inside back (A) over the sofa back, and anchor it with T-pins. Do the same for the outside back (B).

3 Position the seat (C) on the sofa. Matching centers, pin the seat (C) to the inside back (B), creating a tuck-in of 3–6 in (7.5–15cm); trim. Smooth the seat (C) over the sofa seat and down onto the front, anchoring it with T-pins.

4 Anchor the inside arm (D) to the sofa inside arm with T-pins, so that it extends 2 in (5cm) beyond the front edge and the top edge. Pin it to the inside back (A) and to the seat (C), creating tuck-ins of 3–6 in (7.5–15cm) at both; trim. Clip into the seam allowance of the inside back (A) where it forms a right angle at the top of the sofa back. Clip into the seam allowance of the inside arm (D) where it meets the inside back (A) and the seat (C). Repeat for the opposite side.

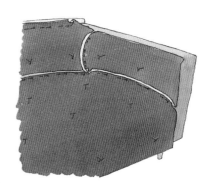

5 Anchor the outside arm (E) to the sofa outside arm with T-pins, so that it extends 2 in (5cm) beyond each edge. Smooth it into place, and check that the grain is at right angles to the floor. Pin it to the outside back (B), clipping into the seam allowance of the outside arm (E) at the top back corner; trim. Repeat for the opposite side.

6 Anchor the side boxing strip (F) to the top of the sofa arm with T-pins, smoothing it down onto the sofa front arm. Pin it to the inside arm (D) and the outside arm (E) along the top and front, clipping into the seam allowances at the front corners of the boxing strip (F); trim.

7 Clip into the seam allowance of the seat (C) at the front corner. Pin the lower portion of the side boxing strip (F) to the front (vertical) part of the seat (C); trim. Repeat the previous step and this step for the opposite side.

8 Pin the side boxing strip (F) to the top (horizontal) part of the inside back (A), behind the clip in the latter; trim. Pin the side boxing strip (F) to the outside back (B); trim. Repeat for the opposite side.

9 Using tailor's chalk, mark each seamline on the wrong side. Remove the T-pins anchoring the fabric to the sofa. Unpin the two seams at the back of the sofa, apart from the top 2 in (5cm), and remove the cover. Using a straightedge, redraw any seamlines that are not straight (without making the cover smaller). Trim all seam allowances to ⅝ in (1.5cm) except for the two back seams (and the lower edge), which should remain 1 in (2.5cm).

10 Unpin one portion of the cover at a time, and repin the pieces with right sides together before moving on to unpin and repin the next section. Check the fit on the sofa, pushing in the tuck-ins.

11 Stitch the seams, leaving ⅝ in (1.5cm) unstitched at the ends, and pivoting at the corners or stitching into them. Stitch only the top 2 in (5cm) of the back seams, as the zippers will be applied there (see step 13). Finish the raw edges of the stitched seams and press them open.

12 Put the cover back on the sofa, and trim the lower edge to ⅝ in (1.5cm). Remove the cover. Make facings from leftover fabric, and face the lower edge between the legs. Turn under a double hem above the legs, clipping into the seam allowance alongside; hand sew. Attach Velcro to the facings and the underside of the sofa.

13 Install a zipper in each of the two unstitched back seams. Put the cover back on the sofa, close the zippers, push in the tuck-ins, and stick the facings to the underside of the sofa.

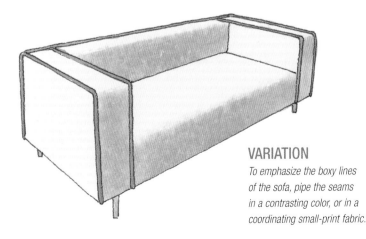

VARIATION
To emphasize the boxy lines of the sofa, pipe the seams in a contrasting color, or in a coordinating small-print fabric.

SNUG ARMCHAIR COVER

IT'S HARD TO SPOT THAT THIS IS ACTUALLY A SLIPCOVER RATHER THAN UPHOLSTERY. HIDDEN FACINGS AND TUCK-INS ARE
THE SECRET OF THE SMOOTH, SNUG FIT AND PROFESSIONAL LOOK.

MATERIALS

Decorator fabric
Matching thread
¼ in (5mm) piping cord
Metal bead fringe
Sew-and-stick Velcro (optional)
Upholstery zipper

TECHNIQUES

Pin-fitting (page 102)
Tuck-ins (page 114)
Corners (page 106)
Piping (page 120)
Zippers (page 112)
Facings (page 114)—optional
Trimmings (page 116)

MEASURING

Measure each section at the widest points, as the
cover will be cut as a series of rectangles. The
inside back (A) and outside back (B) could be treated
as one piece if there is no direction to the fabric.
The fringe should be the chair circumference, plus
3 in (7.5cm). The zipper should be 2 in (5cm)
shorter than the distance from the top of the chair
outside back to the bottom of the seat.

• Depending on the design of the chair, the top
seams on the back and arms could go underneath
the scrolls, instead of halfway around as here.

Inside back (A): *width:* width of inside back, plus
4 in (10cm); *length:* distance from top edge of
outside back, over top of back, and down to seat,
plus 10 in (25.5cm).

Outside back (B): *width:* width of outside back, plus
4 in (10cm); *length:* distance from top of back to
bottom of seat, plus 4 in (10cm).

Seat (C): *width:* width of seat, plus 16 in (40.5cm);
length: distance from inside back to front and down
to bottom of seat, plus 10 in (25.5cm).

Back gusset (D): *width:* distance from inside back
to outside back, plus 4 in (10cm); *length:* distance
from top of back to top of arm, plus 4 in (10cm).

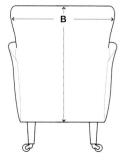

Inside arm (E): *width:* distance from front of arm to inside
back, plus 11 in (28cm); *length:* distance from top of
arm at outside, across top of arm, and down to seat, plus
10 in (25.5cm).

Outside arm (F): *width:* distance from front of arm to
outside back, plus 4 in (10cm); *length:* distance from top
of arm to bottom of seat at outside, plus 4 in (10cm).

Front arm (G): *width:* width of front of scroll, plus 4 in
(10cm); *length:* distance from top of arm to bottom of seat,
plus 4 in (10cm).

Bias strip (H): *width:* 2 in (5cm); *length:* twice the
distances around the back gusset (D) and the front
arm (G), plus twice the distance from inside back to
front of arm, plus 8 in (20.5cm).

TYPICAL YARDAGES

To cover a chair 20 in (51cm) wide and 36 in (91cm)
high, using fabric 54 in (137cm) wide, you would
need about 4 yd (3.6m) of fabric, plus 4 x the
pattern repeat.

CUTTING OUT

Cut 1 x A, 1 x B, 1 x C, 2 x D, 2 x E, 2 x F, and 2 x G, making sure the pattern (or
the nap, if there is one) runs from top to bottom or from back to front. Also make
sure the pattern of each piece will match that of each adjacent piece. Mark the
letters on the pieces.

From the same fabric (or contrasting fabric, if you prefer), cut out and join bias
strips as necessary, to produce 1 x H for piping the seams.

IMPORTANT: Because this cover is snug, all fabric pieces should be placed on the
chair right side up; initially, seams are pinned with wrong sides together (then in
step 10 repinned with right sides together). A seam allowance should be trimmed
to 1 in (2.5cm) once you have pinned together the pieces for that seam; it will be
trimmed to its final ⅝ in (1.5cm) later.

TYPICAL CUTTING LAYOUT FOR 54 IN (137CM) WIDE FABRIC

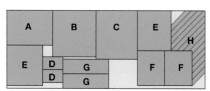

1 Make enough piping to pipe the chair around the back gusset, along the arm, and around the front arm. Use pins to mark the centers of the chair inside back, outside back, and seat, and of the inside back (A), outside back (B), and seat (C) fabric pieces.

2 Place the inside back (A) on the chair, lining up the center with that of the chair. Matching centers, pin the outside back (B) to the inside back (A) across the top at the back; trim. Smooth the inside back (A) over the chair and anchor it with T-pins. Do the same for the outside back (B).

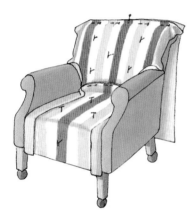

3 Position the seat (C) on the chair. Matching centers, pin the seat (C) to the inside back (A), creating a tuck-in of 3–6 in (7.5–15cm); trim. Smooth the fabric over the chair seat and onto the front, anchoring it with T-pins.

4 Position the inside arm (E) on the chair arm. Anchor the fabric along the top, smooth it down over the arm, and anchor it near the bottom of the arm with T-pins. Pin it to the seat (C) and also to the inside back (A), creating tuck-ins of 3–6 in (7.5–15cm) at both; trim. Clip into the seam allowance of the inside arm (E) where the inside back (A) meets the seat (C). Repeat for the opposite side.

5 Anchor the outside arm (F) to the chair arm and side with T-pins, smoothing it into place and checking that the grain is at right angles to the floor. Pin the outside arm (F) to the inside arm (E) and to the outside back (B); trim. Repeat for the opposite side.

6 With T-pins, anchor the front arm (G) to the front of the chair arm. Pin it to the inside arm (E), making small pleats at the front edge of the inside arm (E) if necessary, to ease in the fullness. Also pin it to the outside arm (F). Trim, clipping into the seam allowance on the curves. Repeat for the opposite side.

7 Clip into the seam allowance of the seat (C) at both front corners. Pin the front arm (G) to the seat (C) as shown. Trim the lower edge of the outside arms (F), front arms (G), seat (C), and outside back (B) 1 in (2.5cm) below the lower edge of the chair seat.

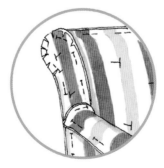

8 Anchor the back gusset (D) to the side of the chair back with T-pins. Pin it to the outside back (B), to the inside back (A), and to the inside arm (E). Trim, clipping into the seam allowance on curves. Clip into the seam allowance of the inside arm (E) where it meets the inside back (A) and the back gusset (D). Repeat for the opposite side.

9 Using tailor's chalk, mark each seamline on the wrong side. Remove the T-pins anchoring the fabric to the chair. Unpin the seam at the back right-hand side of the chair, apart from the top 2 in (5cm), and remove the cover from the chair. Using a straightedge, redraw any seamlines that are not straight (without making the cover smaller). Trim all the seam allowances to ⅝ in (1.5cm) except for the back right-hand seam, which should remain 1 in (2.5cm).

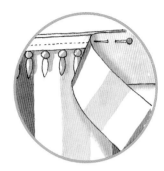

12 The lower edge can be finished by pressing under a narrow hem and then stitching the metal bead fringe to the underside. Or, for a snugger fit, stitch the fringe to the right side of the lower edge, along the hemline (just as you would if attaching piping), then face the lower edges (turning under a narrow hem above the legs and clipping into the seam allowance alongside) and attach Velcro to the facings and the underside of the chair.

10 Unpin one portion of the cover at a time, and repin the pieces with right sides together before moving on to unpin and repin the next section. As you do so, insert a single length of piping into the seams between each back gusset (D) and inside back (A)/outside back (B); between each inside arm (E) and outside arm (F); and between each front arm (G) and seat (C)/inside arm (E)/outside arm (F). Check the fit on the chair, pushing in the tuck-ins.

13 Install the zipper. Now put the cover back on the chair, close the zipper, push in the tuck-ins, and stick the facings (if using) to the underside of the chair.

11 Stitch the seams, leaving ⅝ in (1.5cm) unstitched at the ends (except at the lower edge), and pivoting at corners or stitching into them. Stitch each piped seam as a continuous seam, after stitching the other seams that meet it. Stitch only the top 2 in (5cm) of the back right-hand seam, as the zipper will be applied here (see step 13). Finish the raw edges of the stitched seams and press them open. Clip into the seam allowances (and into the seam allowances of piping) on curves.

VARIATION

Instead of a fringe, attach a box-pleated skirt to the lower edge of the cover.

kitchen & dining room

PLEATED COVER FOR UPHOLSTERED DINING CHAIR

DINING CHAIR SLIPCOVERS IN ALTERNATING COLORS LOOK FABULOUS ARRANGED AROUND A DINING TABLE. THE CLEAN
LINES OF THIS DESIGN ARE PERFECT FOR A STRAIGHT-BACKED UPHOLSTERED DINING CHAIR.

MATERIALS

Decorator fabric
Matching thread
¼ in (5mm) thick piping cord

TECHNIQUES

Piping (page 120)
Pin-fitting (page 102)
Shaping (page 108)
Tuck-ins (page 114)
Corners (page 106)
Inverted pleats (page 108)

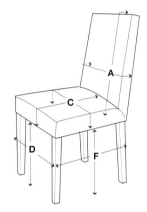

MEASURING

Measure each section at the widest points, as
the cover will be cut as a series of rectangles.
Inside back (A): *width:* distance from one side
edge of outside back, across inside back to other
side edge of outside back, plus 4 in (10cm);
length: distance from top edge of outside back,
over top of back, and down to bottom of seat, plus
10 in (25.5cm).
Outside back (B): *width:* width of outside back,
plus 4 in (10cm); *length:* distance from top of back
to bottom of seat, plus 4 in (10cm).
Seat (C): *width:* distance from bottom of seat
on one side, up and across seat, and down to
bottom of seat on other side, plus 4 in (10cm);
length: distance from inside back to front, and down
to bottom of seat, plus 10 in (25.5cm).
Skirt front (D): *width:* width of chair front beneath
seat, plus 14 in (35.5cm); *length:* distance from
bottom of seat to floor, plus 3 in (7.5cm).
Skirt back (E): *width:* width of chair back beneath
seat, plus 14 in (35.5cm); *length:* distance from
bottom of seat to floor, plus 3 in (7.5cm).
Skirt side (F): *width:* width of chair side beneath
seat, plus 14 in (35.5cm); *length:* distance from
bottom of seat to floor, plus 3 in (7.5cm).
Bias strip (G): *width:* 2 in (5cm); *length:* distance
around chair seat, plus 4 in (10cm).

TYPICAL YARDAGES

To cover a chair 18 in (45.5cm) wide and 37 in (94cm) high, using
fabric 54 in (137cm) wide, you would need about 4 yd (3.6m) of
fabric, plus 5 x the pattern repeat.

CUTTING OUT

Cut 1 x A, 1 x B, 1 x C, 1 x D, 1 x E, and 2 x F, making sure the
pattern (or the nap, if there is one) runs from top to bottom or from
back to front. Also make sure the pattern of each piece will match
that of each adjacent piece. Mark the letters on the pieces.

From the same fabric, cut out and join bias strips as necessary,
to produce 1 x G for piping the seam between the seat and skirt.

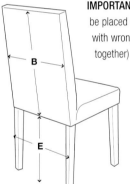

IMPORTANT: Because this cover is snug, all fabric pieces should
be placed on the chair right side up; initially, seams are pinned
with wrong sides together (then in step 8 repinned with right sides
together). A seam allowance should be trimmed to 1 in (2.5cm)
once you have pinned together the pieces for that seam;
it will be trimmed to its final ⅝ in (1.5cm) later.

1 Make enough piping to pipe the chair around
the seat above the skirt. Use pins to mark the
centers of the chair inside back, outside back, and
seat, and of the inside back (A), outside back (B),
and seat (C) fabric pieces.

2 Place the inside back (A) on the chair, lining up the center with that of the
chair. Matching centers, pin the outside back (B) to the inside back (A) across
the top at the back; trim. Make darts at the top corners of the inside back (A).

TYPICAL CUTTING LAYOUT FOR 54 IN (137CM) WIDE FABRIC

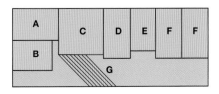

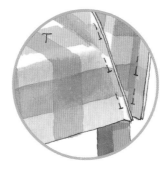

5 Continue pinning the seat (C) to the inside back (A) around the sides, with a diagonal seam sloping downward. (Or, if you prefer, just leave it as a horizontal seam, aligned with the top of the seat.) Trim.

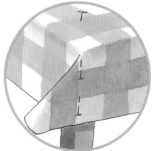

6 Smooth the seat (C) over the chair seat and onto the front and sides, anchoring it with T-pins. Pin a dart at each front corner of the seat (C).

3 Smooth the inside back (A) and outside back (B) over the chair; anchor with T-pins. Smooth the inside back (A) over the sides of the chair back, and continue pinning it to the outside back (B) along the edges of the chair outside back; trim.

7 Using tailor's chalk, mark each seamline and dart on the wrong side. Remove the T-pins anchoring the fabric to the chair, and remove the cover from the chair. Using a straightedge, redraw any seamlines that are not straight (without making the cover smaller). Trim all the seam allowances to ⅝ in (1.5cm).

4 Position the seat (C) on the chair. Matching centers, pin the seat (C) to the inside back (A), creating a tuck-in of 3–6 in (7.5–15cm); trim. Clip into the seam allowances of the inside back (A) and the seat (C) at both bottom corners of the chair inside back, to allow the fabric to wrap smoothly around the corner.

8 Unpin one portion of the cover at a time, and repin the pieces with right sides together before moving on to unpin and repin the next section. Check the fit on the chair, pushing in the tuck-in. Trim the lower edge of the cover so that it is ⅝ in (1.5cm) below the bottom of the seat. Remove the cover from the chair.

9 Stitch the seams, leaving ⅝ in (1.5cm) unstitched at the ends (except at the lower edge), and pivoting at corners or stitching into them. Finish the raw edges and press the seams open. Baste piping along the lower edge of the cover on the right side, allowing for a ⅝ in (1.5cm) seam.

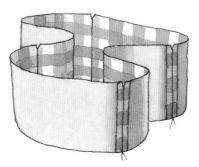

10 With right sides together, stitch the two skirt sides (F) to the skirt front (D) along their side edges with ⅝ in (1.5cm) seams. Stitch the other side edges of the skirt sides (F) to the skirt back (E) in the same way. Finish the seams, and press them open.

12 Remove the cover from the chair, and unpin the corners to allow you to make the pleats. Baste along the length of the pleats; press, then remove the basting. Baste the top of the pleats in place, and repin the corners of the skirt to the cover.

13 Stitch the skirt to the cover with a ⅝ in (1.5cm) seam. Finish the seam, and press. Put the cover on the chair, right side out. Turn up a double 1 in (2.5cm) hem at the lower edge. Remove the cover, press the hem, and then hand sew it. Put the cover back on the chair and push in the tuck-in.

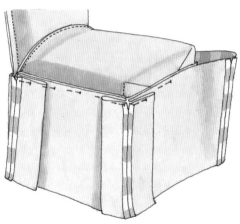

11 Put the cover back on the chair, wrong side out. With right sides together, pin the top edge of the skirt to the lower edge of the cover, lining up the seams on the skirt with the corners of the cover. Form the excess fabric into an inverted pleat at each corner, with the seam at the center of each pleat.

VARIATION

Replace the floor-length skirt with a ruffle (see pages 121–122), and make the outside back in two halves with a button closure (see page 111).

COVER FOR FOLDING CHAIR

SIMPLE SLIPCOVERS CAN MAKE EVEN A MOTLEY GROUP OF FOLDING CHAIRS LOOK LIKE A SET OF SMART DINING CHAIRS. CHOOSE A FABRIC THAT WON'T WRINKLE BADLY WHEN THE COVERS ARE FOLDED UP AND STORED BETWEEN USES.

MATERIALS

Paper for template
Decorator fabric
Matching thread
Twill tape (optional—
    see step 7)

TECHNIQUES

Templates (page 101)
Pin-fitting (page 102)
Shaping (page 108)
Corners (page 106)

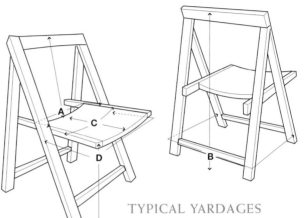

MEASURING

Measure each section at the widest points, as the template for the seat, and the fabric pieces for the skirt and back, are initially cut as rectangles. The measurements allow for ½ in (1cm) ease in the seat.
Inside back (A): *width:* distance from one front leg, around back of seat, to other front leg, plus 4 in (10cm); *length:* distance from top of chair to back of seat, plus 4 in (10cm).
Outside back (B): *width:* distance from one front leg, around back legs, to other front leg, plus 5 in (13cm); *length:* distance from top to floor, plus 2¾ in (6.5cm).
Seat (C): *width:* seat width, plus 1¾ in (4cm); *length:* distance from back to front of seat, plus 1¾ in (4cm).
Skirt (D): *width:* distance from one front leg, around front of seat, to other front leg, plus 1¾ in (4cm); *length:* distance from seat to floor, plus 2¾ in (6.5cm).

TYPICAL YARDAGES

To cover a chair 17 in (43cm) wide and 32 in (81.5cm) high, using fabric 54 in (137cm) wide, you would need about 2¼ yd (2m) of fabric, plus 2 x the pattern repeat.

CUTTING OUT

Using the template (see step 1), cut 1 x C from the fabric. Also cut 1 x A, 1 x B, and 1 x D. Make sure the pattern (or the nap if there is one) runs from top to bottom or from back to front. Also make sure the pattern of each piece will match that of each adjacent piece. Mark the letters on all the pieces.
● If the fabric has no direction to the lengthwise pattern, A and B could be cut out as one piece.

IMPORTANT: Because this cover is loose, all fabric pieces can be placed on the chair wrong side up; seams are pinned with right sides together. A seam allowance should be trimmed to 1 in (2.5cm) once you have pinned together the pieces for that seam; it will be trimmed to its final ⅝ in (1.5cm) later.

TYPICAL CUTTING LAYOUT FOR 54 IN (137CM) WIDE FABRIC

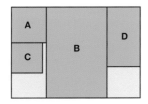

1 From paper, cut out a rectangle to the specified dimensions for the seat (C). Make a shaped template of the chair seat; the template should extend beyond the edges by ⅞ in (2cm). Use the template to cut out the seat (C).

5 Pin the top edge of the skirt (D) to the side and front edges of the seat (C), clipping into the seam allowance of the skirt (D) at the front corners.

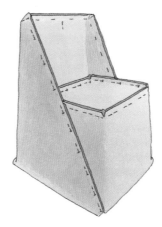

2 With chalk, mark the center of the chair seat and the chair inside back and outside back. With pins, mark the centers of the inside back (A), outside back (B), and seat (C) fabric pieces. Matching the centers, pin the outside back (B) to the inside back (A) across the top.

3 Matching centers, pin the lower edge of the inside back (A) to the back and side edges of the seat (C), stopping when you reach the front legs at each side. Clip the seam allowance of the inside back (A) at the lower back corners.

6 At each side, clip into the seam allowance of the outside back (B), even with the top of the chair seat. Pin the two back edges of the skirt (D) to the outside back (B) beneath the clips, again following the angle of the frame and avoiding pulling the fabric taut; trim.

7 Using tailor's chalk, mark each seamline. Remove the cover from the chair. Using a straightedge, redraw any seamlines that are not straight (without making the cover smaller). Trim seam allowances if necessary. Stitch ⅝ in (1.5cm) seams, leaving ⅝ in (1.5cm) unstitched at the ends (except at the lower edge), and pivoting at the corners or stitching into them. If you wish, stitch pieces of twill tape to the wrong side at the side seams, for tying the cover to the chair legs. Finish the raw edges of the seams, and press the seams open.

4 Pin darts at the top corners of the outside back (B) to shape the fabric over the frame. Pin the inside back (A) and the outside back (B) together at the sides, following the angle of the frame. Avoid pulling the fabric too taut. Trim.

8 Put the cover back on the chair, and turn up a double 1 in (2.5cm) hem along the bottom. Remove the cover. Press the hem and then machine stitch or hand sew it. Put the cover back on the chair, tying the tapes underneath (if using).

VARIATION

Add a single inverted pleat at the center back. Topstitch the upper part of the pleat. Insert the ends of a length of thin cord into the seam at each top corner of the back, and hand sew the center of the cord, along with a tassel, to the seam at the release point of the pleat.

SKIRTED CUSHION FOR WOODEN CHAIR

CUSHIONS ADD COMFORT TO WOODEN DINING CHAIRS, AND DRESSING THE CUSHIONS UP WITH PIPING AND SIMPLE SKIRTS MAKES A SET OF WOODEN CHAIRS LOOK SMART ENOUGH FOR ANY DINING ROOM.

MATERIALS

Decorator fabric (not very
    heavy or thick)
Matching thread
¼ in (5mm) thick piping cord
Purchased bias binding
Heavyweight batting (see step 8)
    or pillow form

TECHNIQUES

Corners (page 106)
Piping (page 120)
Inverted pleats (page 108)

MEASURING

Measure each section at the widest
points, as the cover will be cut as a series of
rectangles. The measurements allow for ½ in
(1cm) ease. The ties are optional.

Seat (A): *width:* width of chair seat, plus 1¾ in
(4cm); *length:* distance from inside back to front of
seat, plus 1¾ in (4cm). If you use a pillow form, or
two layers of batting instead of one, add about ½ in
(1cm) extra to these dimensions.

Skirt front (B): *width:* width of chair seat at front,
plus 13¾ in (34.5cm); *length:* 10¼ in (26cm)—or
19¼ in (49cm) if fabric is very lightweight.

Skirt back (C): *width:* distance between inside of
posts at back, plus 1¼ in (3cm); *length:* 10¼ in
(26cm), plus 2 x thickness of posts—or 19¼ in
(49cm), plus thickness of posts, if fabric is
very lightweight.

Skirt side (D): *width:* distance from inside back
to front of chair seat, plus 7¾ in (19cm); *length:*
10¼ in (26cm)—or 19¼ in (49cm) if the fabric is
very lightweight.

Tie (E): *width:* 2 in (5cm); *length:* 12 in (30.5cm).

TYPICAL YARDAGES

To make a cushion 16 in (40.5cm) square, using
fabric 54 in (137cm) wide, you would need about
1 yd (1m) of fabric, or 1¼ yd (1.1m) if the fabric is
very lightweight, plus 2 x the pattern repeat.

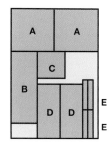

CUTTING OUT

Cut 2 x A, 1 x B, 1 x C, 2 x D, and 4 x E
(optional), making sure the pattern (or
the nap if there is one) runs from top to
bottom or from back to front. Also make
sure the pattern of each skirt piece will
match that of each adjacent piece. Mark
the letters on all the pieces.

1 If you are using ties, press under ¼ in
(5mm) on both long edges and one
end of each tie piece (E). Fold in half
lengthwise, wrong sides together; press,
and then stitch.

2 For the main skirt (which goes around the front and sides), pin one short edge
of the skirt side (D) to one short edge of the skirt front (B), with right sides
together and raw edges even. Stitch a ⅝ in (1.5cm) seam, leaving ⅝ in (1.5cm)
unstitched at the top. Repeat to join the other skirt side (D) to the other short edge
of the skirt front (B). Finish the seam allowances and press the seams open.

3 On the main skirt and on the skirt back (C), press under ¼ in (5mm) and then
⅜ in (1cm) on each end and on the lower edge; stitch. (The skirt back (C) is
deeper than the main skirt. To make sure it's the right length, you could wait to
hem the lower edge until step 7.) Or, if your fabric is very lightweight, the main
skirt and skirt back (C), which are cut longer (see Measuring), should be folded in
half with right sides together, sewn across the ends with ⅝ in (1.5cm) seams, then
turned right side out, folded in half, and pressed, before basting the top edge.

4 Using the bias binding, make enough piping to pipe all four edges of the
cushion. With right sides together, pin and baste the piping around the edges
of one seat (A), clipping into the piping seam allowance at the corners.

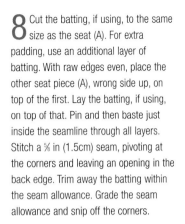

8 Cut the batting, if using, to the same size as the seat (A). For extra padding, use an additional layer of batting. With raw edges even, place the other seat piece (A), wrong side up, on top of the first. Lay the batting, if using, on top of that. Pin and then baste just inside the seamline through all layers. Stitch a ⅝ in (1.5cm) seam, pivoting at the corners and leaving an opening in the back edge. Trim away the batting within the seam allowance. Grade the seam allowance and snip off the corners.

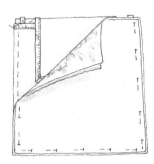

5 If you are using ties, lay the seat (A) on the chair and, with right sides together and raw edges even, pin the unfinished end of each tie to the back edge of the cover at either side of each post. Remove the cover, and stitch the ties in place.

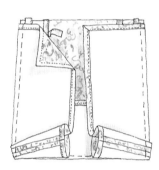

9 Turn the cover right side out and press. Press under the seam allowances of the opening. Insert a pillow form if using. Machine stitch the opening if you have used batting, or slipstitch it if you have used a pillow form. Remove any visible basting, and press the pleats. Put the cushion on the chair and make bows with the pairs of ties, if using.

6 With right sides together and raw edges even, pin the main skirt to the front and side edges of the seat (A), on top of the piping. The hemmed ends of the main skirt should be ⅝ in (1.5cm) from the back edge of the seat (A). Match the seams of the main skirt to the front corners of the seat (A), pinning the excess fabric into an inverted pleat at each front corner; baste across the top of each pleat. Now baste around the entire seam. The seam allowance is ⅝ in (1.5cm), so baste just within this.

VARIATION

Instead of a back skirt and a pleated main skirt, make and attach four long skirt panels as for the skirt back (steps 3 and 7), omitting the piping.

7 With right sides together and raw edges even, pin the skirt back (C) to the back edge of the seat (A). The hemmed ends of the skirt back (C) should be even with the edge of each inside tie. Stitch a ⅝ in (1.5cm) seam. Put the cover on the chair, and, if you haven't done so already, mark the hemline on the lower edge of the skirt back (C) so it is even with that of the main skirt. Remove from the chair, and press under ¼ in (5mm) and then ⅜ in (1cm), trimming first if necessary; stitch.

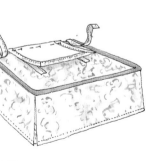

FITTED TABLE COVER

A FLOOR-LENGTH COVER TURNS A MUNDANE TABLE INTO AN ELEGANT SIDEBOARD OR BUFFET. THE COVER WILL ALSO CONCEAL ITEMS STORED UNDERNEATH. GLASS CUT TO FIT THE TABLETOP CAN BE USED OVER THE COVER IF DESIRED.

MATERIALS

Decorator fabric
Contrasting decorator fabric for trim
Matching thread

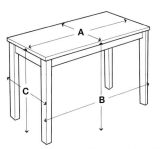

TECHNIQUES

Bias binding (page 116)
Corners (page 106)
Binding an edge (page 118)

MEASURING

The measurements allow for ¼ in (5mm) ease on the width and ½ in (1cm) on the length.

Deck (A): *width:* table width plus 1½ in (3.5cm); *length:* table length plus 1¾ in (4cm).

Skirt side (B): *width:* table height plus ⅝ in (1.5cm); *length:* table length plus ½ in (1cm).

Skirt end (C): *width:* table height plus ⅝ in (1.5cm); *length:* table width plus ¼ in (5mm).

Tie (D): *width:* 4 in (10cm); *length:* 18 in (45.5cm).

Bias strip (E): *width:* 2¾ in (7cm); *length:* 8 x table height, plus 2 x table length, plus 2 x table width, plus 10 in (25.5cm).

TYPICAL YARDAGES

To cover a table 54 in (137cm) long, 32 in (81.5cm) high, and 24 in (61cm) wide, using fabric 54 in (137cm) wide, you would need about 6 yd (5.5m) of the main fabric, plus 4 x the pattern repeat, and about 1 yd (90cm) of the contrasting fabric.

CUTTING OUT

Cut 1 x A, 2 x B, 2 x C, and 16 x D from the main fabric, making sure the pattern (or the nap, if there is one) runs in the same direction. Also make sure the pattern of each piece will match that of each adjacent piece. Mark the letters on the pieces.

From the contrasting fabric, cut out and join bias strips as necessary to produce 1 x E for binding the edges.

• Because none of the bound edges is curved, the binding could be cut on the straight grain instead of on the bias, if it works better with the fabric design.

TYPICAL CUTTING LAYOUT FOR 54 IN (137CM) WIDE FABRIC

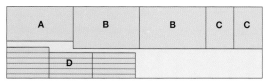

1 Make bias binding from the bias strip (E), turning under ⅝ in (1.5cm) on both raw edges and folding it so that the fold is slightly off center.

2 With right sides together and raw edges even, pin the upper edge of one skirt side (B) to the front edge of the deck (A). Stitch a ⅝ in (1.5cm) seam, leaving ⅝ in (1.5cm) unstitched at the ends.

3 Stitch the upper edge of the other skirt side (B) to the back edge of the deck in the same way as in step 2.

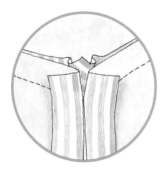

4 Stitch each of the two skirt ends (C) to the remaining raw edges of the deck in the same way as in step 2. Press all the seams open. Check the cover for fit on the table.

5 For the ties, fold each of the fabric pieces (D) in half lengthwise, with right sides together; pin and stitch a ⅜ in (1cm) seam down the long edge and across one end. Snip off the corner of the seam allowance. Turn each tie right side out; press.

6 Pin a tie about a third of the way down one vertical edge of the skirt side (B), with right sides together and raw edges even. Baste in place ½ in (1cm) from the edge. Pin and baste a second tie about the same distance away from the first. Attach two more ties in the corresponding positions on the vertical edge of the adjacent skirt end (C). Attach the remaining ties to the other vertical edges in the same way.

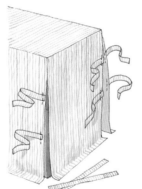

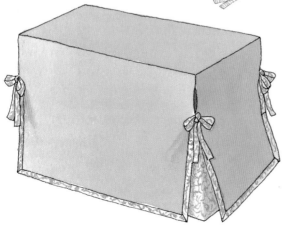

7 Place the cover wrong side up on a flat surface, and at one corner open it out so that the adjacent raw edges of the skirt side (B) and skirt end (C) are in a straight line. Where they meet, stitch them together with a ⅜ in (1.5cm) wide seam, from the edge to the seamline, being careful not to stitch through the deck. Trim the corner of the deck seam allowance.

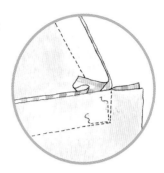

8 Repeat step 7 at the other three corners. Press all four of these short seams open.

9 With the cover right side up on a flat surface, open out the right-hand back corner so that the adjacent vertical edges of the skirt side and skirt end are in a straight line. Pin the deck seam allowance out of the way.

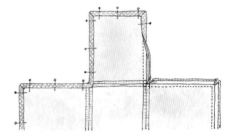

10 Starting at the lower back corner of the skirt, bind the vertical edges and lower edges of the skirt. Use the two-stage method, attaching the narrower side of the binding to the right side of the fabric, turning the binding to the wrong side, and stitching in the ditch from the right side. Take a ⅜ in (1.5cm) seam and miter each corner at the lower edge as you come to it.

11 Slip the cover over the table and make bows with the pairs of ties.

VARIATION

Make inverted pleats at the corners, with underlays in the same fabric as the binding. Attach only one pair of ties, near the top of each pleat. The pleats can be pressed for a crisp look, or left unpressed for a softer effect.

TWO-PIECE COVER FOR DINING CHAIR

A SET OF SHIELD-BACK CHAIRS CAN BE MADE TO LOOK LESS FORMAL AND MORE CHIC WITH A SHAPED TWO-PIECE COVER LIKE THIS. THE DESIGN ALSO ADAPTS WELL TO BALLOON-BACK AND WHEEL-BACK CHAIRS.

MATERIALS
Paper for templates
Decorator fabric (not very
    heavy or thick)
Matching thread
¼ in (5mm) thick piping cord
Purchased bias binding
Batting (see step 1)

TECHNIQUES
Templates (page 101)
Corners (page 106)
Piping (page 120)
Inverted pleats (page 108)

MEASURING
Measure each section at the widest points, as the templates for the seat and back, and the fabric pieces for the skirt, are initially cut as rectangles. The measurements allow for ½ in (1cm) ease in the seat.

• If the back of the seat is flush with the back of the posts, as in the chair on page 38, add the thickness of the posts to the length of the skirt back (C) and deduct it from the length of the seat (A).

Seat (A): *width:* width of chair seat, plus 1¾ in (4cm); *length:* distance from back to front of seat, plus 1¾ in (4cm).

Skirt front (B): *width:* width of chair seat at front, plus 13¾ in (34.5cm); *length:* 5¼ in (13.5cm).

Skirt back (C): *width:* distance between inside of posts at back, plus 1¼ in (3cm); *length:* 5¼ in (13.5cm).

Skirt side (D): *width:* distance from back to front of chair seat, plus 7¾ in (19cm); *length:* 5¼ in (13.5cm).

Tie (E): *width:* 2 in (5cm); *length:* 12 in (30.5cm).

Back (F): *width:* width of shield, plus 1¼ in (3cm); *length:* distance from top to bottom of shield, plus 1¼ in (3cm).

TYPICAL YARDAGES
To cover a chair 20 in (51cm) wide and 36 in (91.5cm) high, using fabric 54 in (137cm) wide, you would need about 1½ yd (1.4m) of fabric, plus 3 x the pattern repeat.

CUTTING OUT
Using the templates (see step 1), cut 2 x A and 2 x F from the fabric. Also cut 1 x B, 1 x C, 2 x D, and 16 x E. Make sure the pattern (or the nap if there is one) runs from top to bottom or from back to front. Also make sure the pattern of each skirt piece will match that of each adjacent piece. Mark the letters on all the pieces.

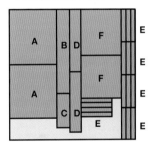

TYPICAL CUTTING LAYOUT FOR 54 IN (137CM) WIDE FABRIC

1 From paper, cut out rectangles to the specified dimensions for the seat (A) and the back (F). Make a shaped template of the chair seat and another of the shield back; the templates should extend beyond the edges of the seat by ⅞ in (2cm) and of the back by ⅝ in (1.5cm). Use these to cut out the fabric pieces for the seat (A) and the back (F). Also cut a piece of batting using each template; for extra padding on the seat (A), cut an additional layer of batting using that template.

5 On the right side of the back cover, pin and baste the piping around the edges of one back (F), clipping into the piping seam allowance at the corners and on curves.

6 With raw edges even, pin pairs of ties down each side edge of the back (F), with some at the top, some near the bottom, and the others halfway between.

7 With raw edges even, lay the second back (F) on top, right side down. Place a layer of batting on top of that. Pin and then baste through all layers. Stitch a ⅝ in (1.5cm) seam all around the edge, leaving an opening at the bottom. Trim away the batting within the seam allowance, grade the seam allowance, clip into it on curves, and snip off corners. Turn the cover right side out, press under the seam allowances of the opening, and stitch.

2 Using the bias binding, make enough piping to pipe the edges of the seat (A) and all around the back (F).

3 Press under ¼ in (5mm) on both long edges and one end of each tie piece (E). Fold in half lengthwise, with wrong sides together; press, and then stitch. Four of the ties are for the seat, and 12 for the back.

8 Fold the underneath tie in each pair away from the edge onto the back, and hand sew it to the back layer about 1 in (2.5cm) from the edge, so the ties can be tied neatly around the wooden rim. Place the seat and back covers on the chair and tie in place.

VARIATION

Omit the pleats and extend the skirt of the seat cover to the floor, adding horizontal spaced tucks to the skirt front. (Allow extra fabric for the tucks, and make them with the folds on the right side of the fabric, prior to assembling the skirt.)

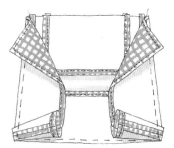

4 Make the seat cover as for the Skirted Cushion for Wooden Chair, steps 2–9 (see pages 38–39), ignoring the instructions for lightweight fabric in step 3.

BUTTONED SEAT COVER

TAILORED SEAT COVERS GIVE A SET OF WOODEN DINING CHAIRS A SMART NEW LOOK FOR VERY LITTLE EXPENSE, AND THE
SEAT PADDING MAKES THE CHAIRS MORE COMFORTABLE.

MATERIALS

Paper for templates
Decorator fabric
Matching thread
Fabric such as
    cotton or muslin
    for lining (optional)
Batting (optional)
Velvet ribbon or braid
6 buttons

TECHNIQUES

Templates (page 101)
Corners (page 106)

MEASURING

Measure each section at the widest points, as the templates are initially cut as rectangles. The measurements allow for ½ in (1cm) ease. The length of the ribbon should be the distance around the chair seat, plus 3 in (7.5cm).

Seat (A): *width:* width of chair seat, plus 1¾ in (4cm); *length:* distance from back to front of chair seat, plus 6⅝ in (16.5cm).

Side (B): *width:* distance from back to front of chair seat, plus 3¼ in (8.5cm); *length:* 6⅜ in (16cm).

Back (C): *width:* width of chair seat, plus 1¾ in (4cm); *length:* 6⅜ in (16cm).

TYPICAL YARDAGES

To cover a chair 20 in (51cm) wide, using fabric 54 in (137cm) wide, you would need about ¾ yd (70cm) of fabric, plus 2 x the pattern repeat. If you line it (see Cutting Out), you would need the same amount of lining fabric (excluding the allowance for a pattern repeat).

CUTTING OUT

From the main fabric, using the templates (see steps 1–3), cut 1 x A, 2 x B (one the mirror image of the other), and 1 x C, making sure the pattern (or the nap, if there is one) runs from top to bottom or from back to front. Also make sure the pattern of each piece will match that of each adjacent piece. Mark the letters on the pieces.

The best way of making this cover is with a lining, as explained here, but you can omit the lining if preferred (see step 8), in which case the seat padding will also have to be omitted.

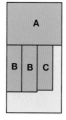

**TYPICAL CUTTING LAYOUT
FOR 54 IN (137CM) WIDE FABRIC**

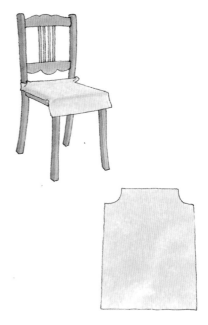

1 From paper, cut out rectangles to the specified dimensions. Make a shaped template of the chair seat; it should extend beyond the edge of the seat by ⅞ in (2cm) at the back and sides, and 5¾ in (14.5cm) at the front. Before cutting it out, redraw the curve around each post ⅝ in (1.5cm) outside the creases. Use this template to cut out the seat (A) from the main fabric, and also from the lining fabric (if using). If you are lining the seat, use the template to cut out some batting to the same dimensions, but excluding the 5¾ in (14.5cm) front extension.

2 Make a paper template for the sides; it should extend beyond the chair at the top by ⅝ in (1.5cm), at the front by ⅞ in (2cm), and at the back by 2⅜ in (6.5cm). Before cutting it out, redraw the curve around each post ⅝ in (1.5cm) outside the creases, so that it meets the curve on the seat template. Use this template to cut out the sides (B)—with one the mirror image of the other—from the main fabric, and also from the lining fabric (if using).

3 Make a paper template for the back; it should extend beyond the chair at the top by ⅝ in (1.5cm) and at the sides by ⅞ in (2cm). Before cutting it out, redraw the curve around each post ⅝ in (1.5cm) outside the creases, so that it meets the curves on the other templates, completing a circle. Use this template to cut out the back (C) from the main fabric, and another from the lining fabric (if using).

4 With right sides together, raw edges even, and the curved edges aligned, pin one main-fabric side (B) to one side of the main-fabric seat (A), aligning the curves. Stitch a ⅝ in (1.5cm) seam, leaving ⅝ in (1.5cm) unstitched at the front edge. Repeat for the other side (B).

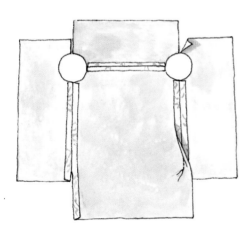

5 With right sides together, raw edges even, and the curved edges aligned, pin the main-fabric back (C) to the back of the main-fabric seat (A) between the curves. Stitch a ⅝ in (1.5cm) seam. Press all three seams open.

6 Pin one side edge of the front extension of the seat (A) to the adjacent short edge of the side (B) as shown, with right sides together and raw edges even, clipping into the seam allowance of the seat (A) at the corner. Stitch a ⅝ in (1.5cm) seam. Repeat for the other side. Press the seams open.

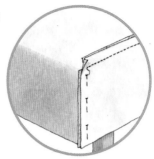

7 With the back edges and side edges even, hand baste the batting to the wrong side of the lining-fabric seat (A), if using, then repeat steps 4–6 for the lining. If you are not lining the cover, skip this step.

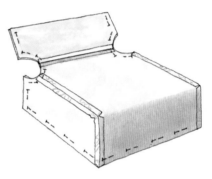

8 If you are lining the cover, place the main fabric and the lining with right sides together, and seams and edges aligned. Pin them together all around the outside, apart from the lower edge of the back (C). Stitch a ⅝ in (1.5cm) seam. Trim the seam allowances to ¼ in (5mm) on the side edges of the back (C). Clip into the seam allowances on the curved seams. If you are not lining the cover, turn under ¼ in (5mm) and then ⅜ in (1cm) around the outside, including the lower edge of the back. Clip into the seam allowances on curves, and then machine stitch.

9 If you have lined the cover, turn the cover right side out and remove the hand basting. Press ⅝ in (1.5cm) to the inside on the lower edge of the main-fabric back (C) and the lining-fabric back (C), and topstitch. If you have not lined the cover, skip this step.

10 Pin ribbon or braid along the lower edge of the back, turning under the ends by ¼ in (5mm); topstitch near both edges of the trim. Sew ribbon or braid to the lower edge of the rest of the cover in the same way. Make three buttonholes at each side of the back (C), and sew corresponding buttons onto the back extensions of the sides (B). Put the cover on the chair, and fasten the buttons to hold it in place.

SHAPED BOX-CUSHION SET FOR DINING CHAIR

WHEN YOU WANT MAXIMUM COMFORT FROM MINIMALIST CHAIRS, MAKE THESE SHAPED BOX CUSHIONS. THEY ARE SO
SIMPLE THAT YOU COULD SEW SOME FOR ALL YOUR DINING CHAIRS IN NEXT TO NO TIME.

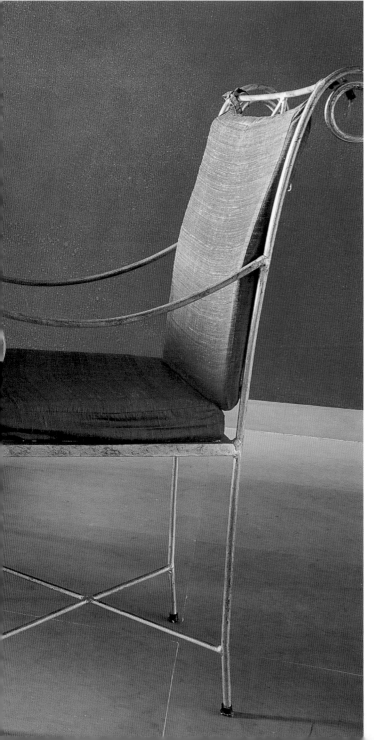

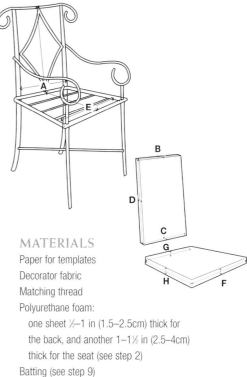

MATERIALS

Paper for templates

Decorator fabric

Matching thread

Polyurethane foam:

  one sheet ½–1 in (1.5–2.5cm) thick for
  the back, and another 1–1½ in (2.5–4cm)
  thick for the seat (see step 2)

Batting (see step 9)

TECHNIQUES

Templates (page 101)

Corners (page 106)

MEASURING

Measure each section at the widest points, as
the templates for the tops/bottoms, and the
fabric pieces for the boxing strips, are initially cut
as rectangles.

Backrest top/bottom (A): *width:* width of chair
back, plus 1¼ in (3cm); *length:* height of back, less
thickness of foam for seat, plus 1¼ in (3cm).

Backrest upper boxing strip (B): *width:* width of
chair back at top, plus 1¼ in (3cm); *length:* thickness
of foam for backrest, plus 1¼ in (3cm).

Backrest lower boxing strip (C): *width:* width of
chair back at bottom, plus 1¼ in (3cm); *length:*
thickness of foam for backrest, plus 1¼ in (3cm).

Backrest side boxing strip (D): *width:* thickness
of foam for back, plus 1¼ in (3cm); *length:*
height of back, less thickness of foam for seat,
plus 1¼ in (3cm).

**TYPICAL CUTTING LAYOUT FOR 54 IN (137CM)
WIDE FABRIC**

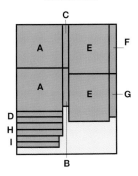

Seat top/bottom (E): *width:* width of chair seat, plus 1¼ in (3cm); *length:* distance from back to front of chair seat, plus 1¼ in (3cm).
Seat front boxing strip (F): *width:* width of chair seat at front, plus 1¼ in (3cm); *length:* thickness of foam for seat, plus 1¼ in (3cm).
Seat back boxing strip (G): *width:* width of chair seat at back, plus 1¼ in (3cm); *length:* thickness of foam for seat, plus 1¼ in (3cm).
Seat side boxing strip (H): *width:* thickness of foam for seat, plus 1¼ in (3cm); *length:* distance from back to front of chair seat, plus 1¼ in (3cm).
Tie (I): *width:* 2 in (5cm); *length:* 18 in (45.5cm).

TYPICAL YARDAGES

To cover a chair 19 in (48cm) wide and 39 in (1m) high, using fabric 54 in (137cm) wide, you would need about 1¼ yd (1.1m) of fabric, plus 3 x the pattern repeat.

CUTTING OUT

Using the templates (see step 1), cut 2 x A and 2 x E from the fabric. Also cut 1 x B, 1 x C, 2 x D, 1 x F, 1 x G, 2 x H, and 2 x I. Make sure the pattern (or the nap, if there is one) runs from top to bottom or from back to front. However, if you prefer, the boxing strips could be cut on the crosswise, rather than lengthwise, grain. Make sure the pattern of each piece will match that of each adjacent piece. Mark the letters on the pieces.

1 From paper, cut out rectangles to the specified dimensions for the backrest top/bottom (A) and seat top/bottom (E). Make a shaped template of the chair back and another of the seat; the templates should extend beyond the edges by ⅝ in (1.5cm). Use these to cut out the backrest top/bottom (A) and seat top/bottom (E) from fabric.

2 Cut off the ⅝ in (1.5cm) seam allowances all around the templates, and use the resulting new templates for the foam. If possible, ask the store selling the foam sheets to precut them to the correct shapes for you, using these templates. If, however, you are cutting the foam yourself, use a felt-tip pen to draw around the templates onto the foam sheets, and then cut them out using sharp dressmaker's shears or an electric or serrated knife sprayed with silicone lubricant.

3 For the ties, press under ¼ in (5mm) on both long edges and both ends of each tie piece (I). Fold in half lengthwise, with wrong sides together; press, and then stitch.

4 Fold the ties in half crosswise. Baste them to the right side of the upper edge of the backrest bottom (A), ⅝ in (1.5cm) from the side edges, with the fold of each tie even with the upper raw edge.

5 With right sides together, raw edges even, and ⅝ in (1.5cm) seam allowances, pin the short ends of the backrest boxing strips (B, C, and D) together into a continuous loop, with the sides (D) alternating with the upper and lower boxing strips (B and C). As you pin each seam, check that it will align with the corners of the backrest top and bottom (A), taking into account the ⅝ in (1.5cm) seam allowances.

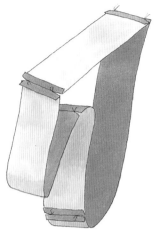

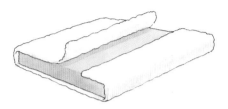

9 Wrap a thin layer of batting around the foam, and slide it into the cover. Slipstitch the opening.

6 Stitch each of the pinned seams, leaving ⅝ in (1.5cm) unstitched at the ends. Press the seams open.

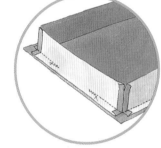

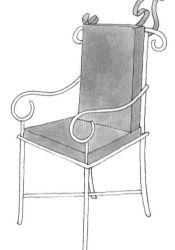

10 For the seat cushion, repeat steps 5–9 for the seat top/bottom (E) and boxing strips (F, G, and H), placing the opening in the seam on the back edge of the seat bottom (E). Put the seat cushion on the chair, and tie the backrest in place on the chair back.

7 With right sides together and raw edges even, pin the boxing strip continuous loop to the backrest bottom (A). Stitch ⅝ in (1.5cm) seams, leaving an opening in the lower edge.

8 Repeat step 7 to attach the boxing strip to the backrest top (A), omitting the opening. Trim the seams and corners, turn the cover right side out, and press. Press under the seam allowances on the opening.

VARIATION

Using the same technique, but with extra ties at the top (and also on the seat cushion) plus piping and slightly thicker foam, make a wide backrest and seat cushion for a garden bench. It will look so smart that you could even bring it into a sunroom, family room, or bedroom.

CHAIR COVER WITH TIED PLEAT AT BACK

TRANSFORM A PLAIN WOODEN CHAIR WITH THIS VERSATILE SLIPCOVER. A BOLDLY STRIPED FABRIC GIVES IT A CHEERFUL, CASUAL LOOK IDEAL FOR A FAMILY ROOM. THE DESIGN CAN ALSO BE ADAPTED TO AN UPHOLSTERED DINING CHAIR BY ADDING A TUCK-IN AT THE BACK OF THE SEAT.

MATERIALS

Decorator fabric
Matching thread
Scrap fabric for "sleeve"
  (see step 1)

TECHNIQUES

Making a "sleeve" (page 103)
Pin-fitting (page 102)
Shaping (page 108)
Corners (page 106)
Inverted pleats (page 108)

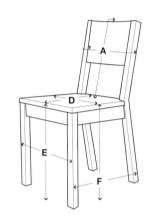

MEASURING

Measure each section at the widest points, as the cover will be cut as a series of rectangles.

Inside back (A): *width:* distance from back edge of one back post, across post, across inside back, and across other post to its back edge, plus 4 in (10cm); *length:* thickness of back posts, plus distance from top of back to top of seat, plus 4 in (10cm).

Left outside back (B): *width:* ½ width of chair back between outside of posts, plus 3 in (7.5cm); *length:* distance from top of back, down outside back to desired height from floor, plus 4 in (10cm).

Right outside back (C): *width:* ½ width of chair back between outside of posts, plus 3 in (7.5cm); *length:* distance from top of back, down outside back to desired height from floor, plus 4 in (10cm).

Seat (D): *width:* width of chair seat, plus 4 in (10cm); *length:* distance from inside back to front of chair seat, plus 4 in (10cm).

Skirt front (E): *width:* distance between outside of front posts, plus 4 in (10cm); *length:* distance from top of seat to desired height from floor, plus 2¾ in (7cm).

Skirt side (F): *width:* distance between outside of front and back posts, plus 4 in (10cm); *length:* distance from top of seat to desired height from floor, plus 2¾ in (7cm).

Pleat underlay (G): *width:* 13¼ in (34cm); *length:* distance from top of back to desired height from floor, plus 4 in (10cm).
Tie (H): *width:* 1½ in (4cm); *length:* 18 in (45.5cm).

TYPICAL YARDAGES

To cover a chair 20 in (51cm) wide and 36 in (91cm) high, using fabric 54 in (137cm) wide, you would need about 3 yd (2.7m) of fabric, plus 4 x the pattern repeat.

CUTTING OUT

Cut 1 x A, 1 x B, 1 x C, 1 x D, 1 x E, 2 x F, 1 x G, and 2 x H, making sure the pattern (or the nap, if there is one) runs from top to bottom or from back to front. Also make sure the pattern of each piece will match that of each adjacent piece. Mark the letters on the pieces.

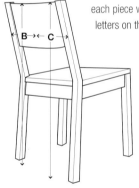

IMPORTANT: Because this cover is quite loose, all fabric pieces can be placed on the chair wrong side up; seams are pinned with right sides together. A seam allowance should be trimmed to 1 in (2.5cm) once you have pinned together the pieces for that seam; it will be trimmed to its final ⅝ in (1.5cm) later.

TYPICAL CUTTING LAYOUT FOR 54 IN (137CM) WIDE FABRIC

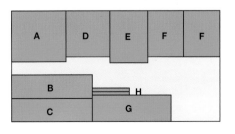

1 From scrap fabric, make a tight-fitting "sleeve" to fit over the back of the chair and give you something to pin to.

2 For each tie (H), press under ¼ in (5mm) on each long edge and one end, and fold in half lengthwise, wrong sides together; press, then stitch.

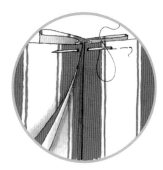

3 With right sides together and raw edges even, pin and stitch one long edge of the pleat underlay (G) to the right-hand long edge of the left outside back (B) with a ⅝ in (1.5cm) seam. Now stitch the other long edge of the underlay (G) to the left-hand long edge of the right outside back (C) in the same way. Press the seams away from the underlay (G). Make an inverted pleat as shown, pressing the pleat and basting across the top.

4 With chalk, mark the center of the chair seat. With pins, mark the centers of the sleeve inside back and outside back, and of the inside back (A) and seat (D) fabric pieces. Matching the centers, pin the outside back (B/C) to the inside back (A) across the top at the back; the center of the pleat should be at the center of the chair back. Make darts at the top corners of the inside back (A) to ease in fullness; trim.

5 Smooth the inside back (A) and outside back (B/C) over the chair and pin them to the fabric sleeve on the chair back. Smooth the sides of the inside back (A) over the posts, and pin it to the outside back (B/C) along the outside back edges of the posts; trim. Clip into the seam allowance of the inside back (A) at each bottom corner.

6 Position the seat (D) on the chair. Matching centers, pin it to the inside back (A); trim.

7 Using tailor's chalk, mark each seamline. Remove the pins anchoring the fabric to the sleeve, and remove the cover from the chair. Using a straightedge, redraw any seamlines that are not straight (without making the cover smaller). Trim all the seam allowances to ⅝ in (1.5cm). Stitch the seams, starting and leaving ⅝ in (1.5cm) unstitched at the ends (except at the lower edge), and pivoting at corners or stitching into them. Finish the raw edges of the stitched seams and press the seams open.

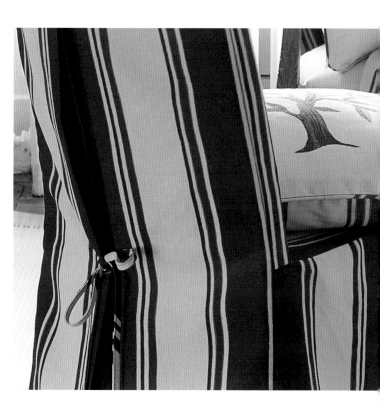

8 Put the cover back on the chair, right side out. With pins, mark on the outside back (B/C), at either side of the pleat, points even with the height of the seat. Trim the seat (D) and the unpinned portions at the sides of the lower edge of the inside back (A) to leave ⅝ in (1.5cm) seam allowances. Pin the skirt front (E) and skirt sides (F) to the cover, and trim the side seam allowances of the skirt pieces to ⅝ in (1.5cm).

9 Unpin the skirt front (E) and sides (F) from the cover, and remove the cover from the chair. Unpick about ⅝ in (1.5cm) of each pleat seam at the points marked in the previous step. Insert the unfinished end of a tie in each of these gaps. Stitch the seams to close the gaps.

10 With right sides together, stitch a skirt side (F) to each side of the skirt front (E) along the side edges. Make ⅝ in (1.5cm) seams, and leave ⅝ in (1.5cm) unstitched at the tops. Finish the raw edges of the seams and press the seams open.

11 Put the cover back on the chair, wrong side out. With right sides together, pin the top edge of the skirt front (E) and skirt sides (F) to the seat (D) and to the portion of the inside back (A) wrapped around the sides of the chair back. The two front seams of the skirt should be lined up with the two front corners of the seat (D). Pin the back edge of each skirt side (F) to the outside back (B).

12 Remove the cover, trim seam allowances if necessary, and stitch ⅝ in (1.5cm) seams, leaving ⅝ in (1.5cm) unstitched at the ends. Finish the raw edges of the seams, and press the seams open.

13 Put the cover back on the chair, and turn up a double 1 in (2.5cm) hem along the bottom. Remove the cover. Press the hem and then machine stitch or hand sew it. Put the cover back on the chair, tying the ties.

VARIATION

Pipe the cover in contrasting fabric. Use this also for the pleat underlay. Instead of ties, make two pointed tabs in this same fabric. Cut four 1¾ x 5 in (4.5 x 13cm) rectangles and stitch them together in pairs, right sides together, with ¼ in (5mm) seams and pointed ends; leave a gap in the seam, turn right side out, and press. Make a buttonhole at each end. Make four covered buttons using the same fabric, and sew one above the other at each side of the pleat. Button the tabs to the cover.

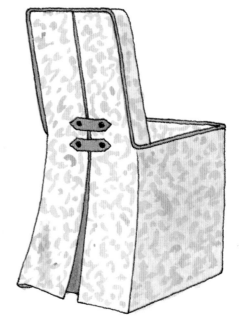

CHAIR COVER WITH DRAPED AND TIED SKIRT

DRESS UP AN OLD CHAIR WITH THIS WHIMSICAL COVER, WHICH WOULD LOOK GOOD IN A FAMILY ROOM OR A GIRL'S BEDROOM. THE DESIGN IS SUITABLE FOR EITHER A HARD CHAIR OR AN UPHOLSTERED ONE.

MATERIALS
Paper for template
Decorator fabric (with no
   direction to lengthwise pattern)
Contrasting decorator fabric
   for trim
Matching thread

TECHNIQUES
Templates (page 101)
Binding an edge
   (page 118)

MEASURING
Measure each section at the widest points, as the template for the back, and the fabric pieces for the skirted seat, boxing strip, and back skirt, are initially cut as rectangles. The measurements allow for ¼ in (5mm) ease in the back.

Inside back (A): *width:* width of chair back, plus 1½ in (3.5cm); *length:* distance from top of back to top of seat, plus 1½ in (3.5cm).

Outside back (B): *width:* width of chair back, plus 1½ in (3.5cm); *length:* distance from top of back to top of seat, plus 1½ in (3.5cm).

Back boxing strip (C): *width:* thickness of chair back, plus 1½ in (3.5cm); *length:* distance from top of chair seat, up side of back and across top, and down to top of seat on other side, plus 2 in (4.5cm).

Skirted seat (D): *width:* width of seat, plus 2 x desired depth of skirt, plus 1¼ in (3cm); *length:* distance from front to back of seat, plus desired depth of skirt, plus 1¼ in (3cm).

Back skirt (E): *width:* distance from inside back, around outside back, to inside back at other side, plus 2 in (4.5cm); *length:* desired depth of skirt, plus 1¼ in (3cm).

Tie (F): *width:* 4 in (10cm); *length:* 18 in (45.5cm).

Bias strip (G): *width:* 2 in (5cm); *length:* distance around chair, plus 8 x desired depth of skirt, plus 2¼ in (6cm).

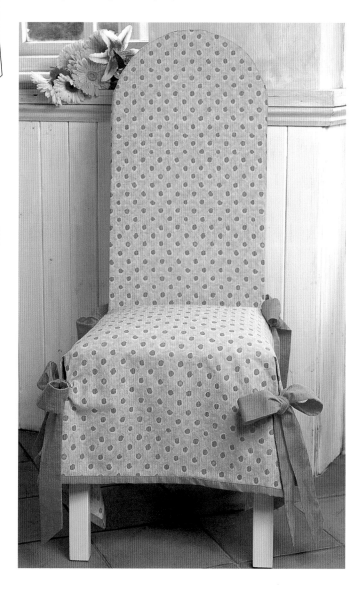

TYPICAL CUTTING LAYOUT FOR 54 IN (137CM) WIDE FABRIC

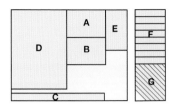

TYPICAL YARDAGES

To cover a chair 19 in (48cm) wide and 35 in (89cm) high, using fabric 54 in (137cm) wide, you would need about 2 yd (1.8m) of the main fabric, plus 2 x the pattern repeat, and about ½ yd (50cm) of the contrasting fabric.

CUTTING OUT

Using the template (see step 1), cut 1 x A and 1 x B from the main fabric. Also cut 1 x C, 1 x D, and 1 x E from the main fabric. Make sure the pattern of each piece will match that of each adjacent piece. Mark the letters on the pieces.

From the contrasting fabric, cut 8 x F, and also cut out and join bias strips as necessary, to produce 1 x G for binding the edges of the skirt.
● Because none of the bound edges is curved, the binding could be cut on the straight grain instead of on the bias.

1 From paper, cut out a rectangle to the specified dimensions for the inside back (A). Make a shaped template of the back; it should extend beyond the edges by ¾ in (1.8cm). Use this to cut out the fabric pieces for both the inside back (A) and the outside back (B).

2 For the ties, fold each of the tie pieces (F) in half lengthwise, with right sides together. Pin and stitch a ⅜ in (1cm) seam down the long edge and diagonally across one end. Snip off the corners of the seam allowances and turn each tie right side out; press. Press under ¼ in (5mm) on both raw edges of the unfinished end of each tie; topstitch.

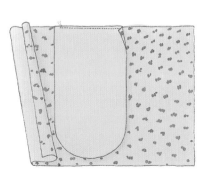

3 With right sides together, pin the lower edge of the inside back (A) to the back edge of the skirted seat (D), with the same amount of fabric extending beyond each side of the inside back (A). Stitch a ⅝ in (1.5cm) seam, leaving ⅝ in (1.5cm) unstitched at the ends. Finish the seam allowances, and press the seam open.

4 Open out the inside back section stitched in the previous step. Press under ¼ in (5mm) and then ⅜ in (1cm) on the back edge of the skirted seat (D) at either end of the seam; topstitch.

5 With right sides together and raw edges even, pin one long edge of the back boxing strip (C) around the edge of the outside back (B), with a ⅝ in (1.5cm) seam. Stitch the seam, leaving ⅝ in (1.5cm) unstitched at the ends. Finish the seam allowances, clip into the seam allowances on curves, and press the seam open.

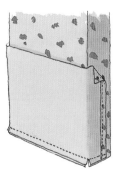

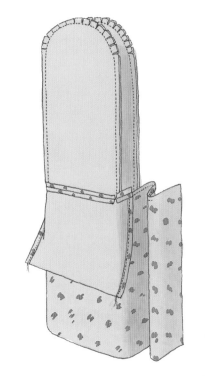

6 Press under ¼ in (5mm) and then ⅜ in (1cm) on the two short ends of the back skirt (E); stitch. With right sides together, pin the top edge of the back skirt (E) to the lower edge of the outside back (B) and boxing strip (C). Stitch a ⅝ in (1.5cm) seam. Clip into the seam allowance of the back skirt (E) opposite the seams joining the outside back (B) and boxing strip (C). Finish the seam allowances. Press the seams open, and open out this outside back section.

7 Place the outside back and inside back sections with right sides together. Pin the inside back (A) to the boxing strip (C) around the outside. Do not pin the skirted seat (D) and the back skirt (E) together, but align their seams. Stitch a ⅝ in (1.5cm) seam. Finish the seam allowances, and clip into the seam allowances on curves. Press the seam open. Turn the cover right side out.

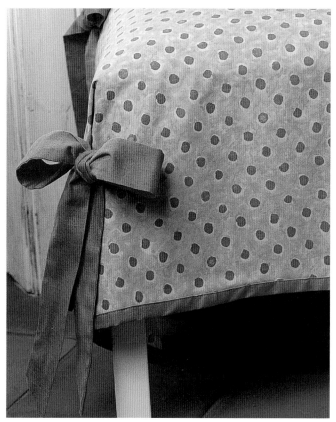

8 Slip the cover onto the chair and mark the positions of the ties (F) on the right side of the fabric. One should be placed at each side edge of the back skirt (E), with another one opposite each of these on the back edges of the other skirt. The remaining two pairs should be positioned at either side of the front legs. Remove the cover, and hand sew the topstitched end of each tie to the fabric.

9 Bind the lower edge of both skirts with the contrasting bias strip (G). Put the cover back on the chair, allowing the skirted seat (D) to drape over the front corners, and making large bows with the pairs of ties.

COVER FOR STUDIO COUCH

THE SIMPLE, MODERN STYLE OF THESE STUDIO COUCHES DICTATES AN EQUALLY STREAMLINED DESIGN FOR THE
SOFT-EDGED BOX-CUSHION COVERS. THE SAME TYPE OF COVER COULD BE MADE FOR MODULAR SEATING.

MATERIALS

Decorator fabric

Matching thread

TECHNIQUES

Pin-fitting (page 102)

Corners (page 106)

MEASURING

Measure each section at the widest points, as the cover will be cut as a series of rectangles. Remove the back from the studio couch when measuring the seat.

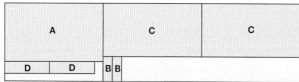

TYPICAL CUTTING LAYOUT FOR 54 IN (137CM) WIDE FABRIC

Back-cover main piece (A): *width:* 2 x height of back, plus 2 x thickness of back, plus 1¼ in (3cm); *length:* length of back, plus 1¼ in (3cm).

Back-cover gusset (B): *width:* height of back, plus 1¼ in (3cm); *length:* thickness of back, plus 1¼ in (3cm).

Seat-cover main piece (C): *width:* distance from front to back of seat, plus thickness of seat, plus 1¼ in (3cm); *length:* length of seat, plus 1¼ in (3cm).

Seat-cover boxing strip (D): *width:* thickness of seat, plus 1¼ in (3cm); *length:* distance from front to back of seat, plus 1¼ in (3cm).

TYPICAL YARDAGES

To cover the back and seat of a studio couch 72 in (183cm) long and 30 in (76cm) wide, using fabric 54 in (137cm) wide, you would need about 6¼ yd (5.7m) of fabric, plus 2 x the pattern repeat.

CUTTING OUT

Cut 1 x A, 2 x B, 2 x C, and 2 x D.

SEAT

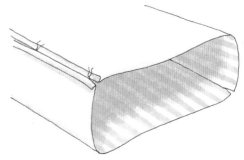

1 Encase the seat cushion in the two seat-cover main pieces (C), wrong sides out, pinning together the long edges at the upper back and lower front edges so that they fit snugly. Trim the seam allowances to ⅝ in (1.5cm). Remove the pinned main pieces (C) and stitch both seams, leaving ⅝ in (1.5cm) unstitched at the ends and leaving a long opening in the back seam. Finish the seam allowances and press the seams open, pressing under the seam allowances on the opening.

BACK

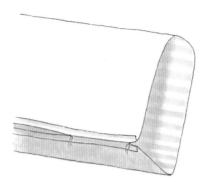

1 Wrap the back-cover main piece (A), wrong side out, around the back cushion, pinning together the two long edges at the lower back edge so that it fits snugly. Trim the seam allowances to ⅝ in (1.5cm). Remove the fabric and stitch the seam, leaving ⅝ in (1.5cm) unstitched at the ends, and leaving a long opening in the seam. Finish the seam allowances and press the seam open. Press under the seam allowances on the opening.

2 Put the main piece (A) back on the cushion, wrong side out, with the seam at the lower back edge. Pin-fit the back-cover gussets (B) on the ends of the back cushion. Trim the seam allowances to ⅝ in (1.5cm).

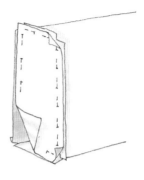

3 With right sides together and raw edges even, pin one back-cover gusset (B) to one end of the main piece (A) with a ⅝ in (1.5cm) seam. The seam on the latter should be at the lower back corner of the gusset (B). Clip into the seam allowance of the main piece (A) at the other three corners. Repeat for the other gusset (B) at the opposite end of the back-cover main piece (A). Stitch the seams.

4 Finish the seam allowances and press the seams open. Turn the cover right side out, insert the back cushion, and slipstitch the opening.

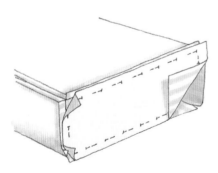

2 With right sides together and raw edges even, pin one end of the joined main piece (C) to one seat-cover boxing strip (D) with ⅝ in (1.5cm) seams. The two seams in the joined main piece (C) should go at the lower front and upper back corners of the boxing strip (D). Clip into the seam allowances of the joined main piece (C) at the other two corners. Repeat for the opposite end and the other boxing strip (D).

3 Stitch the seams, finish the seam allowances, and press the seams open. Turn the cover right side out, insert the seat cushion, and slipstitch the opening closed.

VARIATION

Instead of soft-edged covers, make covers with gussets or boxing strips on all four sides, and pipe the edges in a contrasting color.

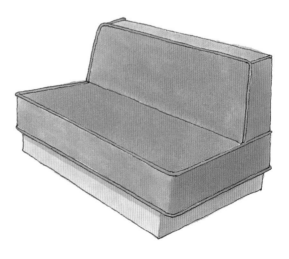

SIMPLE ARMCHAIR COVER

THIS SLIPCOVER IS DESIGNED SO THAT SEAMS DO NOT INTERRUPT THE SMOOTH CURVES AT THE TOP OF THE CHAIR. SEW A
SET, EACH CHAIR IN A DIFFERENT COLOR, TO BRIGHTEN UP A FAMILY ROOM.

MATERIALS

Decorator fabric (with no
   direction to lengthwise pattern)
Matching thread
Upholstery zipper

TECHNIQUES

Pin-fitting (page 102)
Tuck-ins (page 114)
Corners (page 106)
Zippers (page 112)

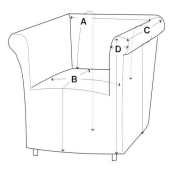

MEASURING

Measure each section at the widest points, as the
cover will be cut as a series of rectangles. The
inside back and outside back are treated as one
piece, as are the inside arm and the outside arm, so
it's important that there is no direction to the fabric.
The zipper should be 2 in (5cm) shorter than the
distance from the top of the chair to the desired
height from the floor.

Back (A): *width:* width of chair outside back, plus
16 in (40.5cm); *length:* distance from seat, up and
around curve of back, and down to desired height of
lower edge, plus 10 in (25.5cm).

Seat (B): *width:* width of seat, plus 16 in (40.5cm);
length: distance from inside back to front of seat
and down to desired height of lower edge, plus
10 in (25.5cm).

Arm (C): *width:* distance from front of arm to
outside back, plus 10 in (25.5cm); *length:* distance
from seat, up and around curve of arm, and down to
desired height of lower edge, plus 10 in (25.5cm).

Front arm (D): *width:* width of front of arm, plus
4 in (10cm); *length:* distance from top of arm to
desired height of lower edge, plus 4 in (10cm).

TYPICAL YARDAGES

To cover a chair 41 in (104cm) wide and 37 in
(94cm) high, using fabric 54 in (137cm) wide, you
would need about 8 yd (7.4m) of fabric, plus 4 x the
pattern repeat.

TYPICAL CUTTING LAYOUT FOR 54 IN (137CM) WIDE FABRIC

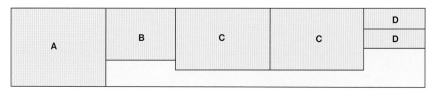

CUTTING OUT

Cut 1 x A, 1 x B, 2 x C, and 2 x D, making sure the pattern of each piece will match that of each adjacent piece. Mark the letters on the pieces.

IMPORTANT: Because this cover is snug, all fabric pieces should be placed on the chair right side up; initially, seams are pinned with wrong sides together (then in step 9 repinned with right sides together). A seam allowance should be trimmed to 1 in (2.5cm) once you have pinned together the pieces for that seat; it will be trimmed to its final ⅝ in (1.5cm) later.

1 Lay the back (A) over the chair back, positioning it so that it is centered between the chair arms and extends 2 in (5cm) below the desired lower edge at the back. Smooth the fabric over the chair inside and outside back, and anchor it with T-pins.

2 Place the seat (B) on the chair seat, so that it is centered between the arms, and extends 2 in (5cm) below the desired lower edge at the front.

3 Pin the seat (B) to the back (A), creating a tuck-in of 3–6 in (7.5–15cm); trim. Smooth the seat (B) over the chair seat, and anchor it with T-pins.

4 Lay one arm (C) over the chair arm, positioning it so that it extends 2 in (5cm) beyond the front edge of the arm, and 2 in (5cm) below the desired lower edge of the chair outside arm. Anchor it at the top with T-pins, smooth it down over the chair inside arm, and anchor it with more T-pins. Repeat for the opposite side.

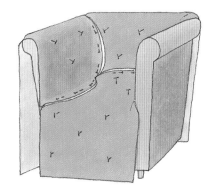

5 Pin the arm (C) to the inside back portion of the back (A), creating a tuck-in of 3–6 in (7.5–15cm). Clip into the seam allowance of the arm (C) at the point where it meets the back (A) and the seat (B). Pin the arm (C) to the seat (B), creating another tuck-in of 3–6 in (7.5–15cm). Trim. Repeat for the opposite side.

6 Smooth the arm (C) over the chair outside arm and side, and anchor it with T-pins. Pin it to the outside-back portion of the back (A); trim, clipping into the seam allowances on the curve. Make a dart in the top edge of the arm (C) near the back corner, to help shape it around the scroll. Repeat for the opposite side.

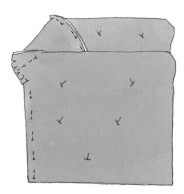

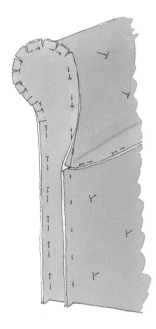

7 With T-pins, anchor the front arm (D) to the front of the chair arm. Pin it to the arm (C), making small pleats at the front edge of the arm (C) if necessary, to ease in the fullness. Trim, clipping into the seam allowance on the curves. Now pin the front arm (D) to the front (vertical) portion of the seat (B), clipping into the seam allowance of the seat (B) at the front corner of the chair seat; trim. Repeat for the opposite side.

8 Using tailor's chalk, mark each seamline on the wrong side. Remove the T-pins anchoring the fabric to the chair. Unpin the seam at the back right-hand side of the chair, apart from the top 2 in (5cm), and remove the cover from the chair. Using a straightedge, redraw any seamlines that are not straight (without making the cover smaller). Trim all the seam allowances to ⅝ in (1.5cm) except for the back right-hand seam, which should remain 1 in (2.5cm).

9 Unpin one portion of the cover at a time, and repin the pieces with right sides together before moving on to unpin and repin the next section. Check the fit on the chair, pushing in the tuck-ins.

10 Stitch the seams, leaving ⅝ in (1.5cm) unstitched at the ends (except at the lower edge), and pivoting at the corners or stitching into them. Stitch only the top 2 in (5cm) of the back right-hand seam, as the zipper will be applied here (see next step). Finish the raw edges of the stitched seams and press them open. Clip into the seam allowances on curves if you have not already done so.

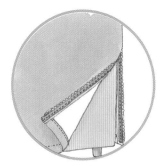

11 Put the cover back on the chair, and turn up a double 2 in (5cm) hem on the lower edge. Remove the cover, press the hem, and machine stitch or hand sew it. Install the zipper in the back right-hand seam; it will curve over part of the scroll at the top. Now put the cover back on the chair, close the zipper, and push in the tuck-ins.

VARIATION

Add interest to the back of the chair by making button loops in a contrasting fabric and inserting pairs of these into the back seams. Cover buttons in the same fabric and attach them near the seamline, for the loops to fit over. Also use this fabric to bind the lower edge of the chair.

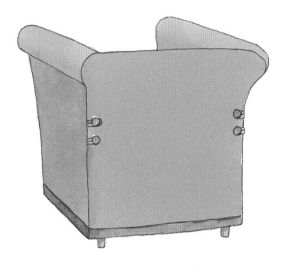

SLIPCOVER FOR DIRECTOR'S CHAIR

TRANSFORM A BORING OR WORN-OUT DIRECTOR'S CHAIR INTO A STYLISH PIECE OF FURNITURE THAT IS PERFECT FOR A FAMILY ROOM BUT WILL ADD A BRIGHT SPLASH OF COLOR OR WHIMSY TO ANY ROOM. THE SLIPCOVER WOULD ALSO BE SUITABLE FOR AN ARMCHAIR OR SOFA OF THE SAME "BOX" SHAPE.

MATERIALS
Decorator fabric
Matching thread

TECHNIQUES
Pin-fitting (page 102)
Corners (page 106)

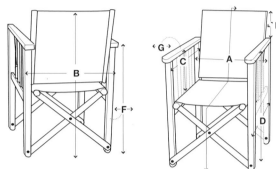

MEASURING
Measure each section at the widest points, as the cover will be cut as a series of rectangles.
• The cover is designed for a chair in which the back fits between the arms.

Front (A): *width:* width of chair back between outside of posts, plus 4 in (10cm); *length:* thickness of back posts, plus distance from top of back to seat, plus distance from back of seat to front, plus distance from seat to floor, plus 4 in (10cm).

Back (B): *width:* width of chair back between outside of posts, plus 4 in (10cm); *length:* distance from top of posts to floor, plus 4 in (10cm).

Inside arm (C): *width:* width of chair side between inside of back post and front of seat, plus 4 in (10cm); *length:* distance between top of arm and seat, plus 4 in (10cm).

Outside arm (D): *width:* width of chair side between outside of back post and front of seat, plus 4 in (10cm); *length:* distance between top of arm and floor, plus 4 in (10cm).

Upper-back boxing strip (E): *width:* thickness of back post, plus 1½ in (4cm); *length:* distance between top of post and top of arm, plus 1½ in (4cm).

Lower-back boxing strip (F): *width:* thickness of arm, plus 1½ in (4cm); *length:* distance between top of arm and floor, plus 4 in (10cm).

Side boxing strip (G): *width:* thickness of arm, plus 1½ in (4cm); *length:* width of chair arm from back to front, plus distance between top of arm and floor, plus 4 in (10cm).

TYPICAL YARDAGES
To cover a chair 20 in (51cm) wide and 38 in (96.5cm) high, using fabric 54 in (137cm) wide, you would need about 3½ yd (3.2m) of fabric, plus 3 x the pattern repeat. To match the pattern crosswise too, or to use fabric 45 in (115cm) wide, would require about 5½ yd (5m), plus 6 x the lengthwise pattern repeat.

CUTTING OUT
Cut 1 x A, 1 x B, 2 x C, 2 x D, 2 x E, 2 x F, and 2 x G, making sure the pattern (or the nap, if there is one) runs from top to bottom or from back to front. Also make sure the pattern of each piece will match that of each adjacent piece. Mark the letters on the pieces.

IMPORTANT: Because this cover is quite loose, all fabric pieces can be placed on the chair wrong side up; seams are pinned with right sides together. A seam allowance should be trimmed to 1 in (2.5cm) once you have pinned together the pieces for that seam; it will be trimmed to its final ⅝ in (1.5cm) in step 11.

TYPICAL CUTTING LAYOUT FOR 54 IN (137CM) WIDE FABRIC

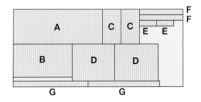

1 With pins, mark the centers of the chair inside back, outside back, and seat, and of the front (A) and back (B) fabric pieces. Place the front (A) on the chair, lining up the centers.

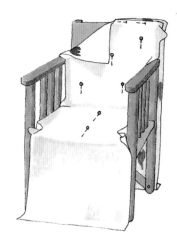

2 Matching the centers, pin the back (B) to the front (A) in a straight line across the top; trim. Smooth the front (A) over the chair inside back and seat, allowing the remainder to drop to the floor at the front. Anchor the fabric to the chair inside back and seat with pins.

3 Pin one vertical edge of the upper-back boxing strip (E) to the back (B), and pin its upper edge to the top portion of the front (A); trim. Clip into the seam allowance of the front (A) at the front corner. Pin the other vertical edge of the boxing strip (E) to the front (A) beneath the clip; trim. Repeat for the opposite side.

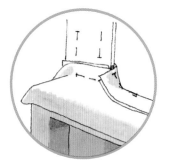

4 Pin the back vertical edge of one inside arm (C) to the lower side edge of the front (A); trim. Lay one side boxing strip (G) along the chair arm. Pin it to the lower edge of the upper-back boxing strip (E) and to the upper edge of the inside arm (C); trim. Repeat for the opposite side.

5 Clip into the seam allowance of the front (A) at the back and front corners. Pin the lower edge of the inside arm (C) to the front (A) between the clips; trim. Repeat for the opposite side.

6 At the inside front corner of one chair arm, clip into the seam allowance of the side boxing strip (G). Pin the inside arm (C) to the side boxing strip (G) beneath this clip; trim. Repeat for the opposite side.

7 Pin the side boxing strip (G) to the front (A) beneath the clip at the front of the chair seat; trim. Repeat for the opposite side.

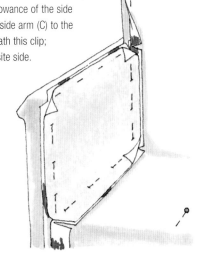

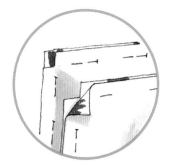

8 Clip into the seam allowance of the side boxing strip (G) at the outside front corner of the chair arm. Pin one outside arm (D) to the side boxing strip (G) along the top of the chair arm and down the front of the chair; trim. Repeat for the opposite side.

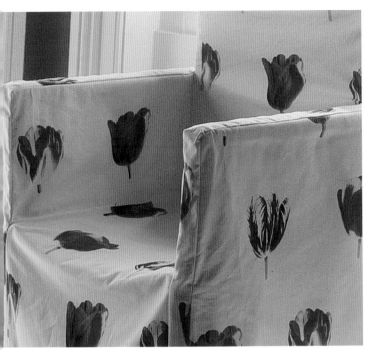

11 Remove the cover from the chair. Using a straightedge, redraw any seamlines that are not straight (without making the cover smaller). Trim the seam allowances to ⅝ in (1.5cm), and the lower hem allowance to 2 in (5cm). Check the fit on the chair.

12 Stitch the seams in the order in which you pinned them, leaving ⅝ in (1.5cm) unstitched at the ends (except at the lower edge), and pivoting at corners or stitching into them. Finish the seams and press them open. Press under a double 1 in (2.5cm) hem around the lower edge; hand sew the hem.

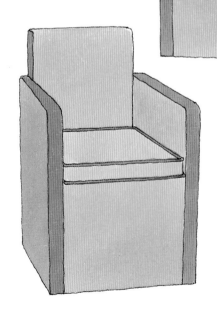

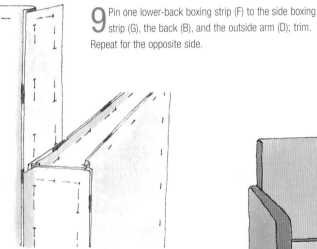

9 Pin one lower-back boxing strip (F) to the side boxing strip (G), the back (B), and the outside arm (D); trim. Repeat for the opposite side.

10 Using tailor's chalk, mark each seamline. Remove the pins anchoring the fabric to the chair. Mark the finished hemline around the lower edge, about ¼ in (5mm) from the floor.

VARIATION

Use a contrasting fabric for all the boxing strips. Add a box cushion in the main fabric, piped in the contrasting fabric.

bedroom

SHORT TAILORED COVER FOR UPHOLSTERED CHAIR

A SHORT SLIPCOVER LIKE THIS IS IDEAL FOR A CHILD'S CHAIR, OR ANY SMALL UPHOLSTERED CHAIR, AS THE COVER DOESN'T SWAMP THE CHAIR. IF YOU USE A NOVELTY FABRIC, POSITION THE IMAGES CAREFULLY FOR MAXIMUM EFFECT.

MATERIALS

Decorator fabric
Matching thread
¼ in (5mm) thick
   piping cord
Purchased bias binding
Sew-and-stick Velcro
Upholstery zipper

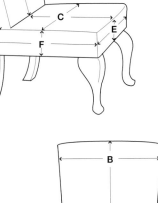

TECHNIQUES

Pin-fitting (page 102)
Tuck-ins (page 114)
Shaping (page 108)
Corners (page 106)
Piping (page 120)
Facings (page 114)
Zippers (page 112)

MEASURING

Measure each section at the widest points, as the cover will be cut as a series of rectangles. The zipper should be 2 in (5cm) shorter than the distance from the top of the chair back at the side, to the bottom of the seat.

Inside back (A): *width:* width of chair inside back, plus 4 in (10cm); *length:* distance from top edge of outside back, over top of back, and down to seat, plus 10 in (25.5cm).

Outside back (B): *width:* width of chair outside back, plus 4 in (10cm); *length:* distance from top of back to bottom of seat, plus 4 in (10cm).

Seat (C): *width:* width of chair seat, plus 4 in (10cm); *length:* distance from inside back to front of chair seat, plus 4 in (10cm).

Boxing strip (D): *width:* thickness of chair back, plus 1½ in (4cm); *length:* distance from top of back to top of seat, plus 4 in (10cm).

Front (E): *width:* width of chair seat, plus 4 in (10cm); *length:* thickness of chair seat, plus 4 in (10cm).

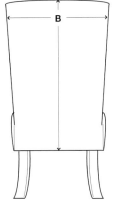

Side (F): *width:* distance from outside back to front of seat, plus 4 in (10cm); *length:* thickness of chair seat, plus 4 in (10cm).

TYPICAL YARDAGES

To cover a chair 19 in (48cm) wide and 34 in (86cm) high, using fabric 54 in (137cm) wide, you would need about 1½ yd (1.4m) of fabric, plus 3 x the pattern repeat.

CUTTING OUT

Cut 1 x A, 1 x B, 1 x C, 2 x D, 1 x E, and 2 x F, making sure the pattern (or the nap, if there is one) runs from top to bottom or from back to front. Also make sure the pattern of each piece will match that of each adjacent piece. Mark the letters on the pieces.

● If your fabric is wide enough, you may be able to cut the front (E) and two sides (F) as one piece.

IMPORTANT: Because this cover is snug, all fabric pieces should be placed on the chair right side up; initially, seams are pinned with wrong sides together (then in step 6 repinned with right sides together). A seam allowance should be trimmed to 1 in (2.5cm) once you have pinned together the pieces for that seam; it will be trimmed to its final ⅝ in (1.5cm) later.

TYPICAL CUTTING LAYOUT FOR 54 IN (137CM) WIDE FABRIC

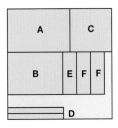

1 Using the bias binding, make enough piping to pipe all the seams. Use pins to mark the centers of the chair inside back, outside back, and seat, and of the inside back (A), outside back (B), and seat (C) fabric pieces.

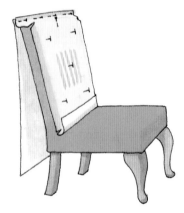

2 Place the inside back (A) on the chair, lining up the center with that of the chair. Matching centers, pin the outside back (B) to the inside back (A) across the top at the back; trim. Smooth the inside back (A) over the chair and anchor it with T-pins. Do the same for the outside back (B). Clip into the seam allowance of the inside back (A) at each top corner and each bottom corner.

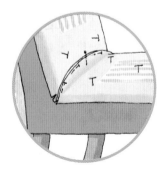

3 Position the seat (C) on the chair. Matching centers, pin it to the inside back (A), creating a tuck-in of 3–6 in (7.5–15cm); trim. Smooth the fabric over the chair seat, anchoring it with T-pins.

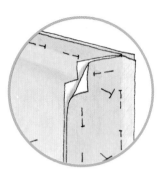

4 Anchor the boxing strip (D) to the side of the chair back with T-pins. Pin it to the inside back (A) and to the outside back (B); trim. Repeat for the opposite side.

5 Using tailor's chalk, mark each seamline on the wrong side. Remove the T-pins anchoring the fabric to the chair. Unpin the seam at the back right-hand side of the chair, apart from the top 2 in (5cm), and remove the cover from the chair. Using a straightedge, redraw any seamlines that are not straight (without making the cover smaller). Trim all the seam allowances to ⅝ in (1.5cm) except for the back right-hand seam, which should remain 1 in (2.5cm).

6 Unpin one portion of the cover at a time, and repin the pieces with right sides together before moving on to unpin and repin the next section. As you do so, insert piping into the seams. At each side of the outside back (B) allow enough extra to pipe to the bottom. Check the fit on the chair.

7 Stitch the seams, leaving ⅝ in (1.5cm) unstitched at the ends (except at the lower edge), and pivoting at corners or stitching into them. For the back right-hand seam, stitch the piping to the boxing strip (D), and stitch only the top 2 in (5cm) of the seam, as the zipper will be applied here (see step 14). Finish the raw edges, clip into the seam allowances on curves, and press the seams open.

8 Put the cover back on the chair, wrong side out, pinning the zipper seam closed. Pin the front (E) and sides (F) to the cover, and trim the seam allowances to ⅝ in (1.5cm), apart from the edge where the zipper will be installed, which should be 1 in (2.5cm).

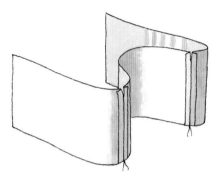

9 Unpin the front (E) and sides (F) from the cover. With right sides together, stitch each side (F) to the front (E) at the side edges with ⅝ in (1.5cm) seams, leaving ⅝ in (1.5cm) unstitched at the tops. Finish the raw edges of the seams, and press the seams open.

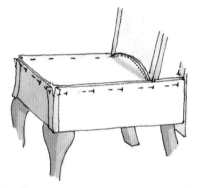

10 With right sides together, pin the top edges of the front (E) and sides (F) to the lower edge of the seat (C) and boxing strip (D). Line up the two seams with the front corners of the seat (C). Pin the back edges of the sides (F) to the outside back (B). Trim all the seam allowances to ⅝ in (1.5cm), apart from the zipper seam, which should be 1 in (2.5cm).

11 Unpin the zipper seam, and remove the cover. Pin the piping into the seams between the outside back (B) and the sides (F). Stitch the left-hand seam, but on the other side just stitch the piping to the back edge of the side (F).

12 Now insert piping into the seam running around the top edges of the front (E) and sides (F), clipping into the piping seam allowance at the corners. Stitch this seam. Finish the raw edges of the stitched seams and press them open.

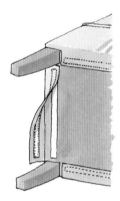

13 Turn under a narrow hem on the lower edge just above the chair legs, clipping into the seam allowance at each side of every leg; hand sew. Face the remainder of the lower edge, and attach Velcro to the facings and the underside of the chair.

14 Install the zipper. Now put the cover back on the chair, close the zipper, push in the tuck-ins, and stick the facings to the underside of the chair.

VARIATION

Stitch pockets (in either matching or contrasting fabric) to the outside back and sides, to hold children's small treasures. For a pencil holder, make the top pocket short and wide, and stitch it to the outside back with vertical lines of stitching about 1½ in (4cm) apart, as well as the usual stitching around the edge.

DAYBED COVER WITH BOLSTERS

A TAILORED COVER, COMBINED WITH A PAIR OF BOLSTERS, TURNS A TWIN BED INTO A SLEEK AND STYLISH DAYBED. THE SCALLOPED LOWER EDGE IS THE FINISHING TOUCH.

MATERIALS

Decorator fabric
   for bedcover
Coordinating decorator
   fabric for bolsters
Matching thread
¼ in (5mm) piping cord
Cardboard for scallop template
Two bolster forms, same length as bed width
Four covered-button kits, 1½ in (4cm) in diameter

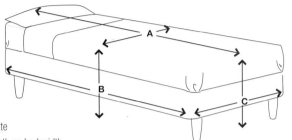

TECHNIQUES

Templates (page 101)
Corners (page 106)
Bias binding (page 116)
Piping (page 120)
Covered buttons (page 111)

MEASURING

Measure the bed with any bedding on it that will be underneath the cover. The measurements allow for 1 in (2.5cm) ease.

Bedcover deck (A): *width:* bed width, plus 2¼ in (5.5cm) *length:* bed length, plus 2¾ in (7cm).

Bedcover skirt side (B): *width:* bed height, plus 2¾ in (7cm); *length:* bed length, plus 2¾ in (7cm).

Bedcover skirt ends (C): *width:* bed height, plus 2¾ in (7cm); *length:* bed width, plus 2¾ in (7cm).

Bolster main piece (D): *width:* bolster circumference, plus 1¼ in (3cm); *length:* bolster length, plus 1¼ in (3cm).

Bolster ends (E): *width:* bolster circumference, plus 1¼ in (3cm); *length:* bolster radius (half of diameter), plus 1¼ in (3cm).

Bedcover bias binding (F): *width:* 2¾ in (7cm); *length:* distance around bed, plus 7 in (18cm).

Bolster bias binding (G): *width:* 2¾ in (7cm); *length:* 2 x bolster circumference, plus 3 in (7.5cm).

TYPICAL YARDAGES

To cover a bed 36 in (90cm) wide, 75 in (190cm) long, and 28 in (71cm) high, using fabric 54 in (137cm) wide, you would need about 8½ yd (7.8m) of fabric, plus 4 x the pattern repeat. If the bed will be against the wall, however, about 6½ yd (6m) of fabric would be enough if you pieced the back skirt section from two strips.

To cover two bolsters, each 36 in (91cm) long and 8 in (20.5cm) in diameter, using fabric 54 in (137cm) wide, you would need about 1½ yd (1.3m) of fabric, plus 2 x the pattern repeat.

CUTTING OUT

FOR THE BEDCOVER cut 1 x A, 2 x B, and 2 x C from the first fabric, making sure the pattern (or the nap, if there is one) runs in the same direction. Also make sure the pattern of each skirt piece will match that of each adjacent piece. (If there is no pattern, the skirt can be cut all in one piece.) Mark the letters on the pieces.

FOR TWO BOLSTERS cut 2 x D and 4 x E from the second fabric.

FOR ALL PIPING cut out and join bias strips from the first fabric as necessary, to produce 1 x F for piping the bedcover, and 2 x G for piping the two bolsters.

TYPICAL CUTTING LAYOUT FOR 54 IN (137CM) WIDE FABRIC

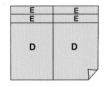

F and G

BEDCOVER

1 Make enough piping to pipe around the top of the bedcover. Pin it to the right side of the deck (A) around all four edges. Machine baste the piping in place, making a ⅝ in (1.5cm) seam and clipping into the seam allowance of the piping at the corners.

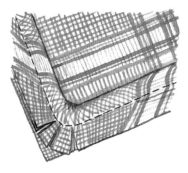

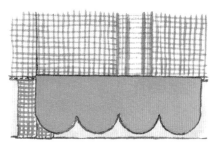

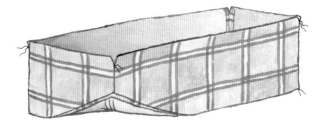

2 With right sides together, stitch a skirt side (B) to a skirt end (C) at the sides with a ⅝ in (1.5cm) seam, leaving ⅝ in (1.5cm) of the seam unstitched at the top. In the same way, join the second skirt side (B) to the other side edge of the skirt end (C), join the second skirt end (C) to the other side edge of the skirt side (B), and finally join the remaining side edges. Press the seams open. Turn under, press, and stitch a single ¼ in (5mm) hem along the lower edge of the skirt.

3 For the scalloped edge, turn 2 in (5cm) to the outside (right sides together) along the lower edge, forming a facing. Make a cardboard template of shallow semicircles 1 in (2.5cm) deep and 2½ in (6.5cm) wide. Starting at a back seam, place the template ¼ in (5mm) away from the folded edge of the facing, and draw around the scallops. Move the template along and repeat the process until the scallops extend around the whole skirt.

BOLSTERS

These directions are for one bolster; make the second in the same way.

1 Make enough piping to pipe around both ends of the bolster. Pin a length to each end of the main piece (D) on the right side, allowing for a ⅝ in (1.5cm) seam allowance; machine baste.

2 With right sides together and raw edges even, join the unpiped edges of the main piece (D) with a ⅝ in (1.5cm) seam (or, for a snug fit, allowing up to double that width of seam and then trimming the seam allowance). Leave an opening in the center of the seam large enough to insert the bolster form. Trim away the piping cord within the seam allowance at each end. Press the seam open.

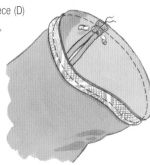

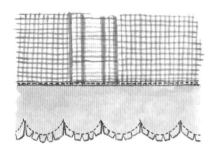

4 Pin and stitch along the marked scallop outline through both layers, pivoting the needle for each new scallop. Now cut ¼ in (5mm) outside the stitching line. Grade the seam allowance, clip the curves, and clip into the "valleys" between the scallops, being careful not to cut through the stitching. Turn the facing to the inside, and press. Slipstitch the edge of the facing to the skirt.

VARIATION

Instead of a scalloped lower edge on the bedcover, add a straight contrast border, and use the same fabric for underlays on inverted pleats at the corners. Make box cushions in the bedcover fabric to lean against the wall, piping them in the border fabric, and make bolsters to match.

5 With right sides together and raw edges even, pin the skirt to the deck, matching the seams to the corners. (If you are making the skirt from one unseamed piece, clip into the seam allowance of the skirt at each corner.) Check that the lower edge will be about ⅜ in (1cm) above the floor, and adjust the seam allowance at the top of the skirt if necessary. Stitch a ⅝ in (1.5cm) seam, pivoting at the corners; trim. Turn the bedcover right side out, and press.

3 Join the short edges of one end piece (E) with right sides together, making a ⅝ in (1.5cm) seam. Press the seam open. Turn under ⅝ in (1.5cm) at one end, press, and stitch. Repeat for other end.

4 With the main piece (D) wrong side out and one end piece (E) right side out, put the end piece (E) inside the main piece (D) so that the right sides are together. Line up the raw edges and the seams, pin, and stitch a ⅝ in (1.5cm) seam. Repeat for the other end. Turn the cover right side out, and press.

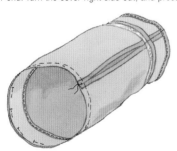

5 Hand sew a double length of gathering thread around both ends, near the edge, and pull up the threads to gather the bolster ends. Fasten the threads securely, and tuck them inside the hole at the center of each end.

6 Using scraps of fabric, make two covered buttons and sew on one at each end to cover the holes and gathering stitches. Insert the bolster form into the cover through the opening. Slipstitch the opening closed.

COVER EXPOSING CHAIR ARMS AND LEGS

FOR AN UPHOLSTERED CHAIR THAT HAS ATTRACTIVE WOODEN ARMS AND LEGS, MAKE A SLIPCOVER THAT DOESN'T COVER UP THESE FEATURES. IT WOULD LOOK LOVELY IN THE BEDROOM—OR, INDEED, IN ANY ROOM.

MATERIALS

Decorator fabric
Matching thread
Sew-on Velcro
14 covered-button kits

TECHNIQUES

Pin-fitting (page 102)
Tuck-ins (page 114)
Shaping (page 108)
Corners (page 106)
Cutaway areas (page 110)
Velcro closures (page 113)

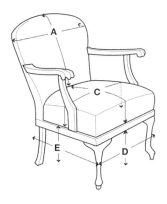

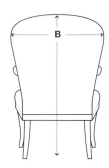

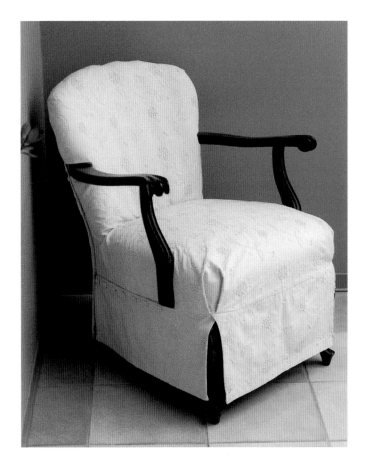

MEASURING

Measure each section at the widest points, as the cover will be cut as a series of rectangles.

Inside back (A): *width:* distance from one side edge of outside back, across inside back to other side edge of outside back, plus 4 in (10cm); *length:* distance from top edge of outside back, over top of back, and down to seat, plus 10 in (25.5cm).

Outside back (B): *width:* width of outside back, plus 4 in (10cm); *length:* distance from top of back to desired height above floor, plus 4 in (10cm).

Seat (C): *width:* distance from bottom of seat on one side, up and across seat, and down to bottom of seat on other side, plus 4 in (10cm); *length:* distance from inside back to front and then down to bottom of seat, plus 10 in (25.5cm).

Skirt front panel (D): *width:* distance between outside of front legs, plus 4 in (10cm); *length:* distance from bottom of seat to desired height above floor, plus 3 in (7.5cm).

Skirt side panel (E): *width:* distance between outside of legs on one side, plus 4 in (10cm); *length:* distance from bottom of seat to desired height above floor, plus 3 in (7.5cm).

TYPICAL CUTTING LAYOUT FOR 54 IN (137CM) WIDE FABRIC

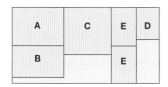

TYPICAL YARDAGES

To cover a chair 26 in (66cm) wide and 33 in (84cm) high, using fabric 54 in (137cm) wide, you would need about 3 yd (2.8m) of fabric, plus 3 x the pattern repeat.

CUTTING OUT

Cut 1 x A, 1 x B, 1 x C, 1 x D, and 2 x E, making sure the pattern (or the nap, if there is one) runs from top to bottom or from back to front. Also make sure the pattern of each piece will match that of each adjacent piece. Mark the letters on the pieces.

IMPORTANT: Because this cover is snug, all fabric pieces should be placed on the chair right side up; initially, seams are pinned with wrong sides together (then in step 6 repinned with right sides together). A seam allowance should be trimmed to 1 in (2.5cm) once you have pinned together the pieces for that seam; it will be trimmed to its final ⅝ in (1.5cm) later, except the Velcro seams (see steps 11–12), which are trimmed to ¾ in (2cm).

1 Use pins to mark the centers of the chair inside back, outside back, and seat, and of the inside back (A), outside back (B), and seat (C) fabric pieces.

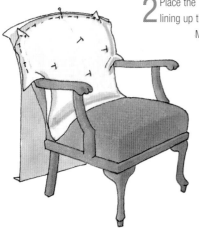

2 Place the inside back (A) on the chair, lining up the center with that of the chair. Matching centers, pin the outside back (B) to the inside back (A) across the top at the back and down the sides as far as the arms; trim. Make darts at the top corners of the inside back (A) to ease in fullness. Smooth the upper portion (above arm-height) of the inside back (A) over the chair and anchor it with T-pins.

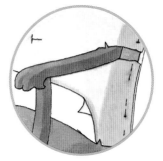

3 Smooth the outside back (B) over the chair back and anchor it with T-pins. Cut away the fabric at each side of the inside back (A) around the arms, leaving ⅜ in (1cm) seam allowances. Smooth the rest of the inside back (A) over the chair and anchor it with T-pins. Pin the inside back (A) to the outside back (B) at the sides beneath the arms; trim. Clip into the seam allowance at the bottom corners of the inside back (A).

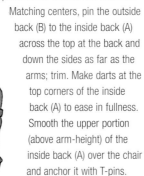

4 Position the seat (C) on the chair. Matching centers, pin the seat (C) to the inside back (A), creating a tuck-in of 3–6 in (7.5–15cm); trim. Smooth the fabric over the chair seat and onto the front, anchoring it with T-pins. Cut away the fabric around the arm supports, leaving a ⅜ in (1cm) seam allowance. Pin two pleats with the folds facing each other at each front corner of the seat (C).

5 Using tailor's chalk, mark each seamline on the wrong side. Remove the T-pins anchoring the fabric to the chair, and remove the cover from the chair. Using a straightedge, redraw any seamlines that are not straight (without making the cover smaller). Trim all the seam allowances to ⅝ in (1.5cm) except for the seams between the inside back (A) and outside back (B) below the arms— these should be trimmed to ¾ in (2cm).

6 Unpin one portion of the cover at a time, and repin the pieces with right sides together before moving on to unpin and repin the next section. Check the fit on the chair, pushing in the tuck-in.

7 Stitch the seams, leaving ⅝ in (1.5cm) unstitched at the ends, and pivoting at corners or stitching into them. When stitching the seam between the inside back (A) and outside back (B), leave the portions below the arms unstitched. Finish the raw edges of the stitched seams and press the seams open. Clip into the seam allowances on curves. Press under the seam allowances on the unstitched seams beneath the arms.

8 From scrap fabric, cut a three-sided facing to fit each cutaway area of the inside back (A) and seat (C). Each side of the facing should be about 1¼ in (3cm) wide. With right sides together and raw edges even, stitch each facing to the corresponding cutaway area with a ⅜ in (1cm) seam, around all three sides. Clip into the seam allowance at each corner, being very careful not to clip through the stitching. Fold the facing to the wrong side of the cutaway area and press. Slipstitch each facing in place on the wrong side.

9 Put the cover back on the chair, right side out. Trim the lower edge of the cover so that it is ¾ in (2cm) beneath the height of the skirt. Pin the skirt front panel (D) and the two skirt side panels (E) to the cover, with a ¾ in (2cm) seam. Trim the back side edge of each skirt side panel (E) to leave ¾ in (2cm) seam allowances. Trim the other side edges and all the lower edges of the skirt panels to leave 1 in (2.5cm) hem allowances.

10 Remove the cover and unpin the skirt panels from the cover. Press under ¼ in (5mm) and then ¾ in (2cm) on both side edges and the lower edge of the skirt front panel (D), and on the front side edge and the lower edge of each skirt side panel (E). Either machine stitch or hand sew these hems, mitering the corners.

11 With right sides together and raw edges even, pin the skirt panels (D and E) to the seat (C). Stitch a ¾ in (2cm) seam starting in front of one cutaway area and stitching across the front to the other cutaway area. Finish the raw edges and press the seam open. Press under the seam allowances on the unstitched portions.

12 Attach Velcro to each side of both unstitched portions of the seam joining the skirt side panels (E) to the seat (C). Do the same for the seams joining the outside back (B) to the inside back (A) and to the skirt side panels (E) beneath the arms. Make covered buttons and attach them below the seamline behind the arm supports. Put the cover back on the chair, fasten the Velcro, and push in the tuck-in.

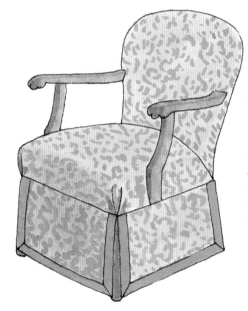

VARIATION

Omit the buttons, and stitch contrasting ribbon, braid, or jumbo rickrack around the side and lower edges of each skirt panel.

COVER FOR WICKER CHAIR

SEW A SIMPLE SLIPCOVER FOR A WICKER CHAIR TO MAKE IT MORE COMFORTABLE AND GIVE IT A COMPLETELY DIFFERENT LOOK.

MATERIALS

Decorator fabric

Matching thread

TECHNIQUES

Pin-fitting (page 102)

Shaping (page 108)

Corners (page 106)

Inverted pleats
  (page 108)

MEASURING

Measure each section at the widest points, as the cover will be cut as a series of rectangles. As the back and arms form a continuous curve, the arms can be deemed to start in line with the struts, or where the curve straightens out. The inside back (A) and outside back (B) can be treated as one piece, and the inside arm (D) and outside arm (E) as one piece (as in the photograph), if there is no direction to the fabric.

Inside back (A): *width:* width of inside back, plus 4 in (10cm); *length:* distance from top edge of outside back, over top of back and down to seat, plus 4 in (10cm).

Outside back (B): *width:* width of outside back, plus 2 in (5cm); *length:* distance from top of back to floor, plus 4 in (10cm).

Front (C): *width:* width of seat, plus 4 in (10cm); *length:* distance from inside back to front and then down to floor, plus 4 in (10cm).

Inside arm (D): *width:* distance from front of arm to inside back, plus 4 in (10cm); *length:* distance from top of arm at outside, down to seat, plus 4 in (10cm).

Outside arm (E): *width:* distance from front of arm to outside back, plus 2 in (5cm); *length:* distance from top of arm to floor, plus 4 in (10cm).

Pleat underlay (F): *width:* 13¼ in (34cm); *length:* height from floor to top of back where arm begins, plus 4 in (10cm).

Tie (G): *width:* 4 in (10cm); *length:* 18 in (45.5cm).

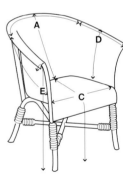

TYPICAL CUTTING LAYOUT FOR 54 IN (137CM) WIDE FABRIC

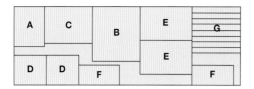

TYPICAL YARDAGES

To cover a chair 26 in (66cm) wide and 27 in (68.5cm) high, using fabric 54 in (137cm) wide, you would need about 4¾ yd (4.3m) of fabric, plus 3 x the pattern repeat.

CUTTING OUT

Cut 1 x A, 1 x B, 1 x C, 2 x D, 2 x E, 2 x F, and 8 x G, making sure the pattern (or the nap, if there is one) runs from top to bottom or from back to front. Also make sure the pattern of each piece will match that of each adjacent piece. Mark the letters on the pieces.

IMPORTANT: Because the cover is quite loose, all fabric pieces can be placed on the chair wrong side up; seams are pinned with right sides together. Apart from the ties (G), a seam allowance should be trimmed to 1 in (2.5cm) once you have pinned together the pieces for that seam; it will be trimmed to its final ⅝ in (1.5cm) later.

1 With chalk, mark the centers of the chair inside back, outside back, and seat. With pins, mark the centers of the inside back (A), outside back (B), and front (C) fabric pieces. Matching the centers, pin the inside back (A) to the outside back (B); trim. Now unpin the pieces.

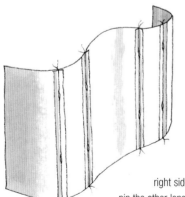

2 With right sides together and raw edges even, pin and stitch one long edge of one pleat underlay (F) to one long edge of the outside arm (E) with a ⅝ in (1.5cm) seam, leaving two 1½ in (4cm) gaps in the seam for the ties (G). Repeat for the other pleat underlay (F) and the other outside arm (E). With right sides together and raw edges even, pin the other long edge of the pleat underlay (F) to one long edge of the outside back (B). Stitch a ⅝ in (1.5cm) seam, leaving 1½ in (4cm) gaps at the same points as the gaps in the previous step. Repeat for the opposite side.

3 Fold each of the fabric pieces for the ties (G) in half lengthwise, with right sides together; pin and stitch a ⅜ in (1cm) seam down the long edge and across one end. Snip off the corner of the seam allowance, and turn each tie right side out; press. Insert the unfinished end of each tie into one of the gaps in the seams. Stitch the seams to close.

4 Pin the outside back (B) to the inside back (A) again across the top. Smooth the pieces over the chair inside back and outside back.

5 Pin long darts around the inside back (A), with the wide part of each dart at the bottom and tapering to the top. The number and size of the darts will depend on the shape of your chair.

6 Pin the back edge of one inside arm (D) to one side edge of the inside back (A); trim. Repeat for the opposite inside arm (D).

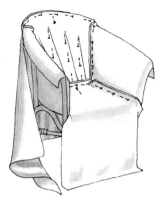

10 Pin the lower side edge of the outside arm (E) to the lower side edge of the front (C); trim. Repeat for the opposite side.

11 Using tailor's chalk, mark each seamline. Mark the finished hemline around the lower edge, about ¼ in (5mm) from the floor.

7 Matching centers, pin the back edge of the front (C) to the lower edge of the inside back (A). Pin the side edges of the front (C) to the lower edges of the inside arms (D), smoothing the rest of the front (C) down over the front of the chair. Trim.

12 Remove the cover from the chair. Using a straightedge, redraw any seamlines and darts that are not straight (without making the cover smaller). Trim the seam allowances to ⅝ in (1.5cm), and the lower hem allowance to 2 in (5cm). Press the pleats, and baste across the tops. Put the cover back on the chair to check the fit.

13 Remove the cover and stitch the darts and then the seams in the order in which you pinned them, starting and stopping ⅝ in (1.5cm) from the ends of the seams (except at the lower edge), and pivoting at corners or stitching into them. Finish the raw edges of the seams, clip into the seam allowances on curves, and press the seams open.

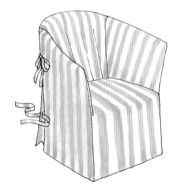

14 Put the cover on the chair, and turn up a double 1 in (2.5cm) hem along the bottom. Remove the cover. Press the hem and then machine stitch or hand sew it. Put the cover back on the chair, tying the ties.

8 Form the pleat underlays (F) into inverted pleats at the back, simply pinning them in place at this stage.

9 Pin the outside arm (E) to the inside arm (D) along the top of the chair arm and down the front of the arm; trim. Repeat for the opposite side. Clip into the seam allowances of the front (C) at the front corners.

VARIATION

For a chair to use in the bathroom, make the cover from two large striped beach towels, omitting the pleats and ties. Use one towel for the inside back/outside back, a piece cut from one long edge of the other towel for a skirt, and the remainder of the towel cut into pieces for the front and inside/outside arms. Instead of sewing conventional seams, overlap the edges, with the finished edge on top, and topstitch. Bind any visible raw edges with tape.

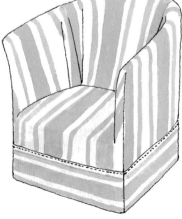

COVER FOR HEADBOARD

A REMOVABLE SLIPCOVER ALLOWS YOU TO CHANGE A HEADBOARD TO MATCH A NEW COLOR SCHEME OR BEDLINEN, AND THE COVER IS PRACTICAL BECAUSE IT EASILY CAN BE REMOVED FOR CLEANING.

MATERIALS

Paper for template
Polyurethane foam, about
   1½ in (4cm) thick (optional)
White glue (optional)
Muslin (optional)
Staple gun (optional)
Decorator fabric
Matching thread
¼ in (5mm) wide piping cord
Sew-and-stick Velcro
   (optional—see step 7)

TECHNIQUES

Templates (page 101)
Corners (page 106)
Piping (page 120)

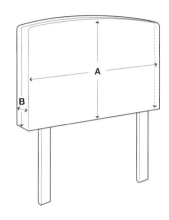

MEASURING

Measure each section at the widest points, as the template for the front and back, and the fabric pieces for the boxing strip, are initially cut as rectangles. The width measurements allow for ½ in (1cm) ease in the front/back (A) and ¼ in (5mm) in the boxing strip.

Front/back (A): *width:* headboard width, plus 1¾ in (4cm); *length:* headboard height, plus 3 in (7.5cm).
Boxing strip (B): *width:* headboard thickness, plus 1½ in (3.5cm); *length:* distance from bottom of headboard, up one end, along top, and down other end, plus 4½ in (11.5cm).
Tie (C): *width:* 3 in (7.5cm); *length:* 18 in (45.5cm).
Bias strip (D): *width:* 2 in (5cm); *length:* 2 x distance from bottom of headboard, up one end, along top, and down other end, plus 9 in (23cm).

TYPICAL YARDAGES

To cover a twin-bed headboard 38 in (96.5cm) wide and 27 in (68.5cm) high, using fabric 54 in (137cm) wide, you would need about 2 yd (1.9m) of fabric, plus 1 x the pattern repeat. To cover a queen-sized-bed headboard 62 in (157cm) wide and 27 in (68.5cm) high, you would need about 3 yd (2.7m) of fabric, plus 2 x the pattern repeat.

TYPICAL CUTTING LAYOUT FOR 54 IN (137CM) WIDE FABRIC

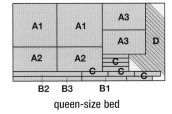

twin bed

queen-size bed

CUTTING OUT

Using the template (see step 1), cut 2 x A from the fabric. Also cut 8 x C. If the headboard is on a twin bed, the fabric will be wide enough not to have to join pieces to cover the whole headboard. For a double bed, you will need to join more than one width to make each A; avoid having a center seam by stitching a center panel with a panel on each side.

From the same fabric, cut out and join strips as necessary to produce 1 x B. As with A, avoid having a center seam—a center piece with pieces on each side is preferable, ideally with the seams lining up with those on A.

From the same fabric (or contrasting fabric or bias binding, if you prefer), cut out and join bias strips as necessary, to produce 1 x D for piping the seams.

1 From paper, cut out a rectangle to the specified dimensions for the front/back (A). Make a shaped template of the headboard from the rectangle; the template should extend beyond the edges by ⅞ in (2cm) at the top and sides. Use the template to cut out the front/back fabric pieces (A).

2 If the headboard padding is worn out or non-existent, remove any old padding and make a template the same size as the headboard, using it to have some thick foam cut. Glue it to the board and stretch muslin over it, stapling it at the back using a staple gun.

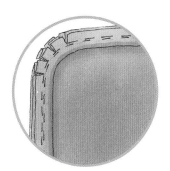

3 Make enough piping to pipe the top and side edges of both the front and back of the headboard. Pin and baste the piping around the top and side edges of the front (A), clipping into the seam allowance of the piping on the curves.

4 For the ties, fold each of the fabric pieces (C) in half lengthwise, with right sides together; pin and stitch a ⅜ in (1cm) seam down the long edge and curving across one end. Snip off the corner of the seam allowances, and turn right side out; press.

5 With right sides together and raw edges even, pin and baste four ties to the side edges of the front (A) in the positions shown.

6 With right sides together, pin the boxing strip (B) to the front (A) around the side and top edges, clipping into the seam allowance of the boxing strip (B) on the curves. Stitch a ⅝ in (1.5cm) seam. Finish the seams, and press.

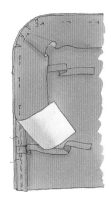

7 Repeat steps 3, 5, and 6 for the back (A), attaching the remaining ties at exactly the same height as those in step 5. Turn the cover right side out and slip it over the headboard. Turn up a double hem on the lower edge. Press the hem; stitch. If desired, stitch Velcro to the inside of the hem, and stick the corresponding strip to the headboard lower edge. Put the cover on the headboard and make bows with the pairs of ties.

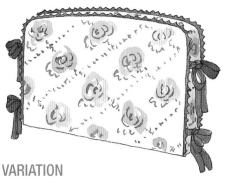

VARIATION

Instead of piping, insert a picot edging in the seams. Choose a headboard fabric that contrasts with the edging, and use the same color for the ties.

sunroom & garden

COVER FOR DECK CHAIR

A QUILTED, PATTERNED REPLACEMENT COVER LIVENS UP A DECK CHAIR AND BRIGHTENS UP THE BACK YARD. IN FACT, IT LOOKS GOOD ENOUGH TO BRING INDOORS, TO USE IN A SUN PORCH OR GARDEN ROOM.

MATERIALS

Decorator fabric in two
  coordinating prints
Matching quilting thread
  or other strong thread
Batting (see steps 4 and 10)
Muslin for making
  pillow form
Furniture tacks and
  hammer, or staple gun
  and heavy-duty staples

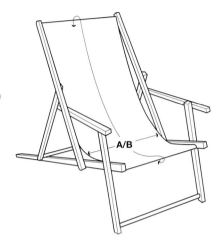

A/B

TECHNIQUES

Quilting (page 123)

MEASURING

Measure the old cover in order to obtain the right curve for the seat.

Front (A): *width:* distance between struts, less 5¾ in (14.5cm); *length:* distance around top rail, along seat, and around bottom rail, plus 1¼ in (3cm).

Back (B): *width:* distance between struts, plus 8¼ in (21cm); *length:* distance around top rail, along seat, and around bottom rail, plus 1¼ in (3cm).

Headrest front (C): *width:* distance between struts, plus 1¼ in (3cm); *length:* 10 in (25.5cm).

Left headrest back (D): *width:* ½ distance between struts, plus 2⅜ in (6cm); *length:* 10 in (25.5cm).

Right headrest back (E): *width:* ½ distance between struts, plus 2⅜ in (6cm); *length:* 10 in (25.5cm).

Tie (F): *width:* 5 in (12.5cm); *length:* 24 in (61cm).

TYPICAL YARDAGES

To make a cover measuring 17 x 51 in (43 x 129cm), using fabric 54 in (137cm) wide, you would need about 1⅔ yd (1.5m) of the first fabric and 2 yd (1.8m) of the second fabric.

CUTTING OUT

Cut 1 x A and 4 x F from the first fabric and 1 x B, 1 x C, 1 x D, 1 x E, and 4 x F from the second fabric, making sure the pattern runs in the same direction. Also make sure the pattern of D and E will match. Cut 2 x C from muslin. Mark the letters on the pieces.

1 For each tie, pin a tie piece (F) in one fabric to another in the other fabric, with right sides together. Pin and stitch a ⅜ in (1cm) seam down one long edge, diagonally across one end, and up the other long edge. Snip off the corners of the seam allowances at the pointed end, turn right side out, and press. Make four ties in this way.

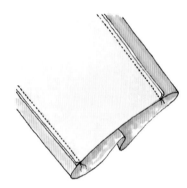

2 Remove the old cover from the deck chair, cutting it away with a sharp craft knife if necessary. With right sides together and raw edges even, pin and then stitch the long edges of the front (A) to the long edges of the back (B) with ⅝ in (1.5cm) seams. Snip off the corners of the seam allowances, and press the seams open.

TYPICAL CUTTING LAYOUT FOR 54 IN (137CM) WIDE FABRIC

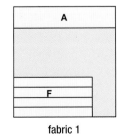

fabric 1

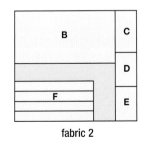

fabric 2

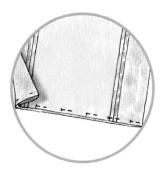

3 With right sides together and the stitched seams equal distances from the sides, pin and then stitch a ⅝ in (1.5cm) seam at the lower end of the cover. Press the seam open. Turn right side out.

4 Cut out a piece of batting to the same dimensions as the stitched cover. Insert the batting inside the cover, making sure it is flat and extends right to the edges. Hand baste through all three layers. At the unstitched end, trim away the batting seam allowance, and press under ⅝ in (1.5cm) on both raw edges of the fabric.

5 Insert the unfinished end of a tie at each side of the unstitched end. Pin and then topstitch the opening.

6 The central portion of the cover (made from the first fabric) is quilted, but the portions on either side (made from the second fabric) are not. Choose a quilting stitch pattern appropriate to the pattern of the fabric—a diagonal grid is used here—and topstitch the central portion to quilt it. Also stitch in the ditch along the two seams joining the central portion to the strips. Remove the basting.

7 Press under and stitch a double ¼ in (5mm) hem on the inner edges of the left and right headrest backs (D and E). With right sides up, overlap these edges by about 2½ in (6.5cm), so that the headrest back (D/E) will be the same width as the headrest front (C). Baste the two headrest backs (D and E) together at the top and bottom, and treat as one piece (D/E).

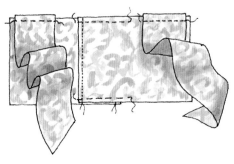

8 With right sides together and raw edges even, baste the unfinished ends of two ties at the top edge of the headrest back (D/E), each ⅝ in (1.5cm) from the side edges.

9 With right sides together and raw edges even, pin the headrest front (C) to the headrest back (D/E) around all four edges. Stitch a ⅝ in (1.5cm) seam, pivoting at corners. Snip off the corners of the seam allowances, turn right side out, and press.

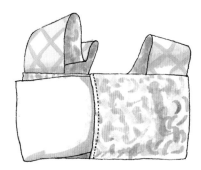

10 For the pillow, stitch the two muslin pieces together around all four sides, right sides together, with a ⅝ in (1.5cm) seam, leaving an opening in one edge. Turn right side out. Stuff with batting, and slipstitch the opening closed. Insert the pillow into the headrest cover.

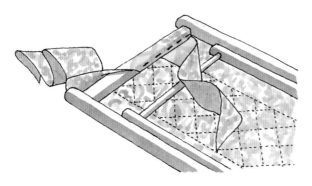

11 Lay the cover wrong side up on the floor, and put the deck chair frame on top. Wrap one end of the cover over the rail. Starting at the center and working outward, attach the end of the cover to the rail using furniture tacks and a hammer, or a staple gun. Repeat at the opposite end, but check the fit after securing the cover with just a few tacks or staples. Adjust if necessary, then finish attaching the cover.

12 Tie the headrest to the cover with big bows.

SIMPLE COVER FOR WOODEN CHAIR

A SIMPLE COTTON COVER WITH A SHORT SKIRT LIVENS UP A PLAIN WOODEN CHAIR AND YET IS PRACTICAL ENOUGH FOR A SUNROOM OR KITCHEN. THE DESIGN IS ALSO SUITABLE FOR AN UPHOLSTERED DINING CHAIR IF A TUCK-IN IS ADDED.

MATERIALS

Decorator fabric such as gingham
Matching thread
Scrap fabric for "sleeve" (see step 1)

TECHNIQUES

Making a "sleeve" (page 103)
Pin-fitting (page 102)
Shaping (page 108)
Corners (page 106)
Inverted pleats (page 108)

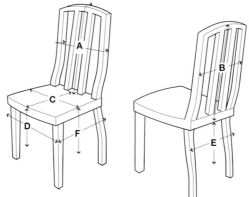

MEASURING

Measure each section at the widest points, as the cover will be cut as a series of rectangles.

Inside back (A): *width:* distance from back edge of one back post, across post, across inside back, and across other post to its back edge, plus 4 in (10cm); *length:* thickness of back posts, plus distance from top of back to top of seat, plus 4 in (10cm).

Outside back (B): *width:* width of chair back between outside of posts, plus 4 in (10cm); *length:* distance from top of back, down outside back to bottom of seat, plus 4 in (10cm).

Seat (C): *width:* width of chair seat, plus 4 in (10cm); *length:* distance from inside back to front of chair seat, plus 4 in (10cm).

Skirt front (D): *width:* distance between outside of front posts, plus 4 in (10cm); *length:* distance from top of seat to desired height from floor, plus 2¾ in (7cm).

Skirt back (E): *width:* distance between outside of back posts, plus 12 in (30.5cm); *length:* distance from top of seat to desired height from floor, plus 2¾ in (7cm).

Skirt side (F): *width:* distance between outside of front and back posts, plus 6 in (15cm); *length:* distance from top of seat to desired height from floor, plus 2¾ in (7cm).

Pleat underlay (G): *width:* 7¼ in (18cm); *length:* distance from top of seat to desired height from floor, plus 2¾ in (7cm).

Tie (H): *width:* 2½ in (6.5cm); *length:* 15 in (38cm).

TYPICAL CUTTING LAYOUT FOR 54 IN (137CM) WIDE FABRIC

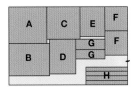

TYPICAL YARDAGES

To cover a chair 26 in (66cm) wide and 33 in (84cm) high, using fabric 54 in (137cm) wide, you would need about 2½ yd (2.2m) of fabric, plus 3 x the pattern repeat.

CUTTING OUT

Cut 1 x A, 1 x B, 1 x C, 1 x D, 1 x E, 2 x F, 2 x G, and 4 x H, making sure the pattern (or the nap, if there is one) runs from top to bottom or from back to front. Also make sure the pattern of each piece will match that of each adjacent piece. Mark the letters on the pieces.

IMPORTANT: Because this cover is quite loose, all fabric pieces can be placed on the chair wrong side up; seams are pinned with right sides together. A seam allowance should be trimmed to 1 in (2.5cm) once you have pinned together the pieces for that seam; it will be trimmed to its final ⅝ in (1.5cm) later.

1 From scrap fabric, make a tight-fitting "sleeve" to fit over the back of the chair, to give you something to pin to.

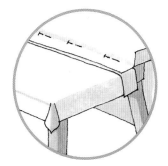

2 With chalk, mark the center of the chair seat. With pins, mark the centers of the sleeve inside back and outside back, and of the inside back (A), outside back (B), and seat (C) fabric pieces. Matching the centers, pin the outside back (B) to the inside back (A) across the top (at the back edges of the posts); trim. Make darts at the top corners of the inside back (A) to ease in fullness.

3 Smooth the inside back (A) and outside back (B) over the chair and pin them to the fabric sleeve on the chair back. Smooth the sides of the inside back (A) over the posts, and pin to the outside back (B) along the outside back edges of the posts; trim. Clip into the seam allowance of the inside back (A) at each bottom corner.

4 Position the seat (C) on the chair. Matching centers, pin it to the inside back (A); trim.

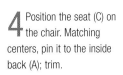

5 Using tailor's chalk, mark each seamline. Remove the pins anchoring the fabric to the fabric sleeve, and remove the cover from the chair. Using a straightedge, redraw any seamlines that are not straight (without making the cover smaller). Trim all the seam allowances to ⅝ in (1.5cm). Stitch the seams, leaving ⅝ in (1.5cm) unstitched at the ends, and pivoting at corners or stitching into them. Finish the raw edges of the stitched seams and press the seams open.

6 Put the cover back on the chair, wrong side out. Trim the seat (C), the outside back (B), and the unpinned portions at the sides of the lower edge of the inside back (A), to leave ⅝ in (1.5cm) seam allowances. Pin the skirt pieces (D, E, and F) to the cover. Trim the seam allowances on the side edges at the front of the chair to ⅝ in (1.5cm).

7 Unpin the skirt pieces (D, E, and F) from the cover, and remove the cover from the chair. With right sides together, stitch a skirt side (F) to each side of the skirt front (D) along the side edges. Make ⅝ in (1.5cm) seams, leaving ⅝ in (1.5cm) unstitched at the top.

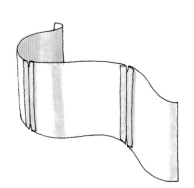

8 With right sides together, stitch a pleat underlay (G) to each skirt side (F) with a ⅝ in (1.5cm) seam, but leaving a 1⅛ in (3cm) gap in the stitching for the tie (H). Stitch the skirt back (E) to the pleat underlays (G) in the same way, leaving gaps at the same height as the other ones. Finish the raw edges of the seams and press the seams open.

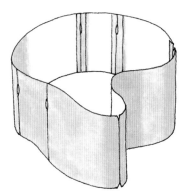

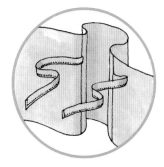

9 For each tie (H), press under ¼ in (5mm) on each long edge and one end, and fold in half lengthwise, wrong sides together; press, then stitch. Insert the unfinished ends of the ties (H) in the gaps left in the underlay seams (see step 8). Stitch the gaps in the seams.

10 With right sides together, pin the top edge of the skirt front (D) and sides (F) to the seat (C) and to the portion of the inside back (A) wrapped around the sides of the chair back. Line up the two front seams of the skirt with the two front corners of the seat (C). Pin the top edge of the skirt back (E) to the lower edge of the outside back (B). Clip into the center of each underlay (G), and line up these clips with the back corners, forming the excess fabric into an inverted pleat at each corner. Baste and press along the length of the pleats, then remove the basting.

11 Stitch with a ⅝ in (1.5cm) seam; finish the seam, and press. Put the cover back on the chair. Turn up a double 1 in (2.5cm) hem along the bottom. Remove the cover. Press the hem and then machine stitch or hand sew it. Put the cover back on the chair, tying the ties.

VARIATION

Lengthen the skirt, put pleats at the corners, and use a contrasting fabric for the underlays and ties.

LINING AND CUSHIONS FOR RATTAN CHAIR

A PADDED LINING COMBINED WITH BACK AND SEAT CUSHIONS TURNS A HARD, SCRATCHY RATTAN OR WICKER CHAIR INTO A COMFY ARMCHAIR FOR A SUNROOM OR KITCHEN.

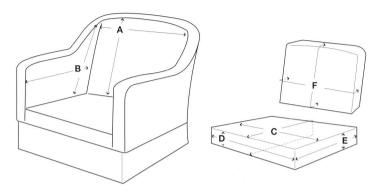

MATERIALS

Paper for templates
Decorator fabric
Matching thread
Batting (see Padded Lining, step 1,
   and Cushions, steps 5 and 7)
Covered-button kit (optional)
Strong quilting thread (optional)
Polyurethane foam, about 4 in (10cm) thick
   (see Cushions, step 1)

TECHNIQUES

Templates (page 101)
Corners (page 106)
Button tufting (page 123)

MEASURING

Measure each section at the widest points, as the templates for the lining, and the fabric pieces for the cushions, are initially cut as rectangles. When measuring to the top of the chair, actually measure to just beneath the rim if there is one.

Lining back (A): *width:* width of chair inside back, plus 1¼ in (3cm); *length:* distance from seat to top of chair at center back, plus 1¼ in (3cm).

Lining side (B): *width:* distance from front of arm to inside back, plus 1¼ in (3cm); *length:* distance from top of arm to seat, plus 1¼ in (3cm).

Seat cushion main piece (C): *width:* width of chair seat, plus 1¼ in (3cm); *length:* 2 x distance from front to back of seat, plus thickness of foam, plus 1¼ in (3cm).

Seat cushion back boxing strip (D): *width:* width of chair seat, plus 1¼ in (3cm); *length:* thickness of foam, plus 1¼ in (3cm).

Seat cushion side boxing strip (E): *width:* thickness of foam, plus 1¼ in (3cm); *length:* distance from front to back of seat, plus 1¼ in (3cm).

Back cushion (F): *width:* width of chair inside back, plus thickness of foam, plus 1¼ in (3cm); *length:* height of chair back, plus thickness of foam, plus 1¼ in (3cm).

TYPICAL CUTTING LAYOUT FOR 54 IN (137CM) WIDE FABRIC

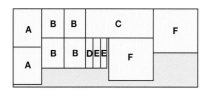

TYPICAL YARDAGES

To cover a chair 32 in (81.5cm) wide and 36 in (91.5cm) high, using fabric 54 in (137cm) wide, you would need about 3⅔ yd (3.4m) of fabric, plus 4 x the pattern repeat.

CUTTING OUT

Using the templates (see Lining, step 1), cut 2 x A and 4 x B (two mirror images of the other two) from the fabric. Also cut 1 x C, 1 x D, 2 x E, and 2 x F. Make sure the pattern (or the nap, if there is one) runs from top to bottom or from back to front. Also make sure the pattern of each piece will match that of each adjacent piece. Mark the letters on the pieces.

PADDED LINING

1 From paper, cut out rectangles to the specified dimensions for the lining back (A) and lining side (B). Make shaped templates of the chair back and side from these, with a ⅝ in (1.5cm) seam allowance all around. Use the templates to cut out the fabric pieces, making two lining sides (B) the mirror image of the other two. Also cut out one piece of batting from the template for the lining back (A) and two from the template for the lining sides (B).

2 With right sides together and raw edges even, pin one lining side (B) to one side edge of the lining back (A). Pin the mirror-image lining side (B) to the other side edge of the lining back (A). Stitch ⅝ in (1.5cm) seams, trim the seam allowances, and press the seams open. Repeat for the remaining lining pieces.

CUSHIONS

1 Buy the foam pieces precut to the correct dimensions. If any shaping is necessary, such as trimming the top corners of the back cushion, give the supplier a template.

3 With right sides together and raw edges even, pin the short ends of the side boxing strips (E) to either end of the back boxing strip (D) with ⅝ in (1.5cm) seam allowances. Check that the seams will align with the back corners of the main piece (C), taking into account the ⅝ in (1.5cm) seam allowances on it. Stitch the seams, leaving ⅝ in (1.5cm) unstitched at the ends. Press the seams open.

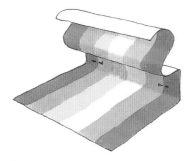

2 The seat cushion is a soft-edged box cushion, which has a boxing strip at the sides and back but not at the front; the main fabric piece (C) is used for both the top and bottom. Fold this piece in half crosswise and mark the center point with pins at both edges; unfold.

4 Fold the boxing strip (D/E) in half lengthwise and mark the center points with pins at each end; unfold. With right sides together and raw edges even, pin one end of the boxing strip (D/E) to the edge of the portion of the main piece (C) that will be at the front of the seat, matching the marked center points. Repeat for the other end of the boxing strip (D/E). Matching the seams to the back corners of the main piece (C), pin the long edges of the boxing strip (D/E) to the main piece (C). Stitch a ⅝ in (1.5cm) seam, leaving an opening in the back edge.

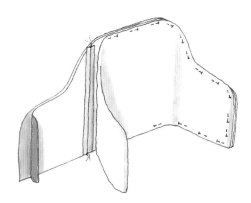

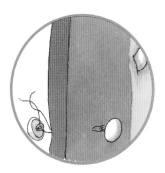

3 Place the two lining back/sides (A/B) with right sides together and raw edges even. Position the batting pieces on top. Pin and baste all three layers together. Stitch ⅝ in (1.5cm) seams around the edges, leaving an opening in the bottom edge of the lining back (A). Trim away the batting within the seam allowances, snip off the corners, grade the seams, and clip the curves. Press the seam allowances open. Turn the lining right side out, press under the seam allowances of the opening, and slipstitch it closed.

4 To help keep the layers together, topstitch along the seamlines joining the lining back (A) and sides (B). If you wish, you can also hand quilt it with button-tufting, using covered buttons, at regular intervals. If you wish to anchor the lining to the chair, take hand stitches through the rattan or wicker at these points. (However, this is difficult if the rattan or wicker is thick or densely woven, and makes removing the lining for cleaning more difficult.) Remove the visible basting.

5 Repeat step 4 to attach the remainder of the main piece (C) to the boxing strip, but without an opening. Trim all the seam allowances, snip off the corners, and press. Turn the cover right side out, and press under the seam allowances on the opening. Wrap a layer of batting around the foam, insert it into the cover, and slipstitch the opening.

7 With the cover wrong side out, pull the top and bottom apart at each corner, centering the seams one over the other. With a fabric marker, mark a point on the seamline a distance from the corner equal to half the thickness of the foam. Draw a line at right angles to the seamline at this point; the whole line will be the same length as the thickness of the foam. Pin and stitch along the line, as shown. Trim the original seam allowance, but don't trim off the excess fabric. Turn the cover right side out. Wrap a layer of batting around the foam, insert it into the cover, and slipstitch the opening.

6 The back cushion is a mock box cushion, which has no boxing strip. With right sides together and raw edges even, pin the two cushion pieces (F) together on all four sides. Stitch ⅝ in (1.5cm) seams, leaving an opening in the back edge. Snip off the corners of the seam allowances. Press the seams open.

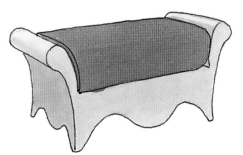

VARIATION

Make a cushion like the seat cushion but with the back as well as the front soft-edged (see pages 60–61), and use it on a matching wicker footstool.

TWO-PIECE COVER FOR DIRECTOR'S CHAIR

DIRECTOR'S CHAIRS PROVIDE PERFECT SEATING IN A SUNROOM OR OUTSIDE ON A DECK. IF THE BACKS AND SEATS ARE WORN OUT—OR JUST PLAIN DREARY—REPLACING THEM WILL GIVE THE CHAIRS A NEW LEASE ON LIFE.

MATERIALS

Heavyweight canvas
Matching quilting
   thread or other
   strong thread
Furniture tacks
   and hammer, or
   staple gun and
   heavy-duty staples
Large grommets

TECHNIQUES

Grommets (page 112)

MEASURING

Measure the old cover in order to obtain the right curve for the seat.

Back (A): *width:* distance around one back rail, across back of frame, and around other back rail, plus 2 in (5cm); *length:* height of back rails (or less, if you prefer), plus 2 in (5cm).

Seat (B): *width:* distance around one seat rail, across seat, and around other rail, plus 2 in (5cm); *length:* length of seat rails, plus 2 in (5cm).

TYPICAL YARDAGES

To cover a chair 27 in (68cm) wide, using fabric 54 in (137cm) wide, you would need about 1 yd (90cm) of fabric.

CUTTING OUT

Cut 1 x A and 1 x B. Mark the letters on the pieces.

**TYPICAL CUTTING
LAYOUT FOR 54 IN
(137CM) WIDE FABRIC**

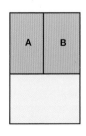

4 Turn the chair over and attach the other side of the seat (B) in the same way, but check the fit on the chair after securing it with only a few tacks or staples. Adjust if necessary, and secure with more tacks or staples.

1 Remove the old cover, cutting it away with a sharp craft knife if necessary.

5 The back (A) is attached to the inside of the two back rails in the same way, with the folded edges along the rear inside edges. Where there are bolts or screws in the rails that will go through the fabric, remove them, then remove the rails from the frame. Wrap the fabric edge around the rail as in step 3, and mark the positions of the holes on the fabric, on both sides of the rail. Repeat for the opposite side. Check the fit on the chair. Apply grommets at these positions. Attach the fabric to one rail as in step 3, making sure the grommets align with the holes.

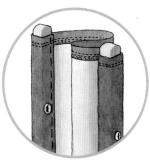

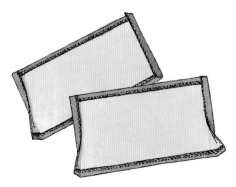

2 Zigzag all the raw edges of the new material after cutting out the pieces. Press under a 1 in (2.5cm) single hem on the top and bottom edges of the back (A), and on the front and back edges of the seat (B). Stitch the hems with a double row of stitching. Now press under a 1 in (2.5cm) single hem on each side edge, but do not stitch.

6 Attach the back (A) to the other rail with just a few tacks or staples, check the fit, and then secure it with more tacks or staples. Reassemble the chair.

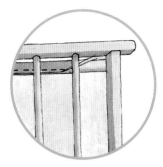

VARIATION

If the arms interrupt the back rails on your director's chair, you could make casings at each side of the back (with double rows of stitching, for strength) and simply slide these over the rails. Each casing will need to be about 2½–4 in (6–10cm) wide.

3 Lay the chair on its side, and wrap one side of the seat (B) over one side rail, so that the turned-under edge of the seat (B) is on the underside of the rail, with the folded edge of the fabric parallel to the edge of the rail. Working outward from the center, secure it with furniture tacks or staples.

FABRICS

You will probably fall in love with a fabric because of its color, pattern, and texture, but its aesthetic appeal also depends on more pragmatic considerations. Choose the material carefully and then don't skimp on the preparation.

PRACTICALITY

Although slipcover fabric doesn't have to be quite as sturdy as upholstery fabric, durability is still a key factor. Medium-weight, firmly woven decorator fabric is usually the best choice. Avoid thick or very heavy material, particularly if the cover requires stitching through a lot of layers. Also avoid rough-textured fabrics, which will wear out more quickly and attract more dirt than smoother ones.

Take into account whether the cover will need to be washable. Obviously the fabric must be colorfast and shrink-resistant if you plan to wash it.

If a fabric has a glaze (such as chintz fabric) or a special finish (for example, to give it body or make it flame-retardant or more resistant to creasing, stains, dirt, mildew, or fading or rotting in the sun), dry cleaning is preferable because washing could remove the finish.

The fiber content is another important factor. Natural fibers, such as cotton and linen, may shrink when washed and will wrinkle easily, whereas synthetic fibers are less prone to shrinking and wrinkling but will tend to attract dirt. A fabric made from a blend of fibers may offer the optimum combination of qualities.

Information about care, special finishes, and fiber content is given on the

LEFT In the right fabric, even the simplest design can look fantastic. Here, check gingham chair-back covers are constructed in the same way as a scrap-fabric "sleeve" used in making a full-size cover (see page 103).

label and is also sometimes printed on the selvages (the finished edges running the length of the fabric).

PATTERN AND PILE

Unless you are experienced at making slipcovers, it's advisable to avoid fabric with a large pattern, because the motifs may have to be positioned carefully on each piece, and the pattern will certainly have to be matched at the seams (see page 104). Choose instead a solid-colored fabric or one with a very small, random pattern. Remember, too, that a pattern with a large repeat (the lengthwise distance from one point in the motif to the same point in the next one) will require more fabric than one with only a short repeat, making the cover more expensive. If you do choose a patterned fabric, make sure that the pattern follows the grain line fairly accurately. Slight variations are sometimes unavoidable, but check that they will not be noticeable.

Some fabrics have a direction, which means that the pattern isn't the same if turned the opposite way around. Fabrics with a pile (such as velvet, velveteen, or chenille) or a nap (such as flannel) also have to run in the same direction, because the surface looks much richer one way up. When stitching pile fabrics, baste first, and stitch with the pile, rather than against it. You can press the seam allowances but you should steam, not press, the fabric.

TRIAL RUN

If you are using a fabric that requires careful pattern matching or is expensive, or if the slipcover will be a tricky design, consider making the cover first from muslin, then using the muslin pieces as a pattern for the slipcover. It may be quicker and cheaper in the long run.

PREPARING FABRIC

If the old upholstery has a noticeable texture or is a very dark or bright color, it may be necessary to line the slipcover to prevent the old fabric showing through.

If the fabric—and any piping cord you are using—is not preshrunk, preshrink it yourself, either by washing it and ironing it dry, or by sending it to a dry cleaner for steaming. Press it from the wrong side.

Before measuring or cutting out your fabric pieces, you have to "square" the fabric, by cutting the edges so that they are at right angles to each other, following the pattern if there is one.

Squaring unpatterned fabric

1 Lay the fabric out on a large, flat, clean surface, supporting the excess fabric if necessary to prevent its weight from pulling it out of shape. Check for flaws.

2 Snip into the selvage near the end and pull out a crosswise thread. Cut along the line where the thread was. Repeat for the opposite end.

3 Line up one leg of a carpenter's square with the cut edge, placing it so the other leg is near the selvage. If the selvage is not parallel to it, mark a line with tailor's chalk along the carpenter's square, and cut along this. If it is parallel, simply trim off the selvage, since it can make seams pucker. Repeat for the opposite edge.

Squaring patterned fabric

1 For fabric such as a plaid, which has a crosswise element (running from one selvage to the other), begin as for step 1 of squaring unpatterned fabric.

2 Now cut along the line of the crosswise pattern, even if the pattern is slightly off-grain. Repeat for the opposite end.

3 Finish squaring the fabric as for step 3 of squaring unpatterned fabric.

FABRIC PLACEMENT

This can be a simple task or quite a complex one, depending on the design of the cover and the fabric pattern.

MEASURING

Each project in this book indicates what fabric pieces are needed for that particular slipcover. These sections start out as rectangles of fabric (see Pin-fitting, page 102) or of paper (see Templates, below), which are then adjusted to fit the piece of furniture, say a chair. The length of the rectangle is the length of that part of the chair at the widest point, plus allowances (see below), and the width is the width of that part of the chair at the widest point, plus allowances. Therefore, you need to measure each section of the chair, as described for each project under Measuring and illustrated in the measurement diagrams for that project. Make a note of all the dimensions.

• Be careful not to mix up length and width when laying out the pieces. Length refers to the measurement along the length of the fabric (parallel to the selvages), while width refers to the measurement across the fabric width (from selvage to selvage). Occasionally the length is less than the width.

• When measuring a very curved surface—such as back legs that curve backward, or a concave chair back—on which the cover will follow the curve, be sure to measure along the surface, rather than simply from one edge to the other in a straight line. Use a flexible tape measure or a piece of string to do this.

ALLOWANCES

Added to each dimension are allowances for seams, hems, ease (to allow the cover to slip on), closures, pleats, and tuck-ins. The total allowance for each dimension is specified under Measuring in the directions for each project.

Pin-fitting allowances

For the projects that involve fabric rectangles that are pin-fitted on the chair (see page 102), the allowances are quite generous, to give you some room for maneuver.

• About 2 in (5cm) has been allowed for ease and each seam or hem, even though the seam allowances are usually trimmed to ⅝ in (1.5cm) ultimately.

• Tuck-ins—extra fabric that is tucked down into the crevices around the seat, arms, and wings, to hold the cover in place—should be 3–6 in (7.5–15cm), depending on the chair or sofa, and so 6 in (15cm) has been allowed for them. If your chair or sofa has only shallow tuck-in crevices, you could allow a little less.

• Pleats are assumed to be 6 in (15cm) wide, but they could be slightly smaller if you prefer.

Template allowances

For the projects that involve paper rectangles that are made into templates (see below), which are then used to cut out the exact fabric shapes, the dimensions are more precise.

• Usually, seam allowances are ⅝ in (1.5cm), hem allowances 2 in (5cm).

• Ease, if any, is about ¼–½ in (5mm–1cm).

Skirts and cushion covers

• For pleated skirts sewn onto pin-fitted covers, no ease is allowed.

• For cushion and bolster covers, no ease is allowed; in fact, for a very plump effect, the cover can be slightly smaller than the cushion or bolster itself.

YARDAGES

Once you have carefully worked out the overall dimensions of each piece, look at the Cutting Out directions for the project to find out how many of each piece you need to cut. You can then work out how much fabric you will need. The Typical

Cutting Layouts show how the pieces might fit on your fabric, and the Typical Yardages information gives the total yardage based on those layouts. But obviously both of these will depend on the dimensions of your cover and your fabric.

The simplest method is to draw your own cutting layout, writing in the dimensions of each piece and then adding them up. Drawing it to scale on graph paper can make it easier to visualize and is also a good way of double-checking your calculations.

The most common width for decorator fabric is 54 in (137cm), but some fabrics may be only 48 in (122cm) wide, while others can be 60 in (152cm) or more in width. If you are slipcovering a sofa or very wide chair, an extra-wide fabric may prevent you from having to join widths.

Allowing for the pattern

When devising your own cutting layouts, take into account any pattern on the fabric.

• Because large motifs need to be positioned carefully (see below), they will waste fabric across the width, so allow for this when working out how many pieces you can fit across the width.

• To calculate how much extra to allow for the repeat, count the pieces along the length, subtract one, and multiply this figure by the size of the repeat. For example, the cutting layout on page 12 shows 10 pieces along the length. If the repeat is, say, 4 in (10cm), you'd multiply 9 (i.e., 10 minus 1) by 4 in (10cm), and so allow 36 in (90cm) extra. (For each project, an allowance for the repeat is given in Typical Yardages, but this relates only to the Typical Cutting Layout.)

TEMPLATES

Whereas upholstered furniture and T-cushions (shaped like the letter T) lend themselves to pin-fitting (see page 102), covers for wooden chairs and tables, and also other cushions, are generally easier to make using templates. These are simply paper patterns for a shape. In this book templates incorporate a seam allowance.

Making a template for a chair seat

1 Cut out a rectangle to the specified dimensions and place it on the chair. Fold it back on itself along the struts at the back, or downward between the posts, depending on the design of the chair, creating a crease at the back edge of the seat. Fold it downward at the front and sides of the seat to crease these edges as well.

2 Measure the specified seam allowance outside the creases and draw this outer shape around the seat with a pencil or pen. Also mark the positions of the ties at the sides of the struts.

3 Fold the template in half from left to right, and adjust the outline so it is the same on both halves to make the template symmetrical. Cut out the shape.

PATTERN MATCHING

Pattern matching and the positioning of motifs obviously have to begin before the pieces are cut out. Adjacent pieces have to match, with the pattern positioned symmetrically and any dominant motifs centered on the inside back, outside back, seat, and front. The positioning on the front arm of a scroll-arm style is important, too.

The pattern runs down the chair inside back, over the seat, and then down to the floor. It also runs down the outside back. Similarly, it runs from the top of each arm down the inside arm, and also down the outside arm, at the same time matching the inside back and outside back respectively. Any seat and back cushions need to match as well. You can see why beginners are advised not to tackle fabric with a pattern that requires matching.

• Pin-fitting the pieces on the chair with the fabric right side out makes precise pattern matching and positioning of motifs easier because you can see the pattern clearly.

• Remember that it is the seamlines you will be matching, not the raw edges. When there is a seam allowance of 4 in (10cm) or more, that can make a big difference.

ABOVE If you are not experienced at making slipcovers, choose a fabric with no pattern or only a small, unnoticeable one, like this ticking.

Direction

If the pattern has a direction (see page 99), it should run from top to bottom and from back to front. For this reason, the inside and outside arms (and also the inside and outside back) of slipcovers in directional fabric should be separate. If they were done as one piece, the inside arm would be upside down. And if the top of the arm had a slope, cutting the inside arm and outside arm as one piece could prevent the pattern on the inside arm from being at right angles to the seat.

JOINING FABRIC WIDTHS FOR SOFAS

If your fabric is positioned on a sofa in the conventional way, running from top to bottom, it will probably be too narrow. Therefore panels need to be stitched together to create one piece that is wide enough. This will be necessary for the inside and outside backs, the seat, the front, and any skirt.

The seams on all these should align with each other and also with the edges of any cushions. It's preferable to avoid having a center seam and instead to have three panels joined to form the wide piece. (The exception to this is where there are just two seat and two back cushions on a sofa, in which case a center seam joining two panels is preferable.) Where it is necessary to join panels to form a single piece (say, A), the panels are shown in the Typical Cutting Layouts as, for example, A1, A2, A3.

CUTTING OUT AND MARKING

Whether you are drawing around templates or measuring and then drawing rectangles straight onto the fabric, work on the right side of the fabric, using tailor's chalk and taking into account the pattern if necessary (see page 101). For vertical pieces, allow for the fact that the grain of the fabric should be at right

angles to the floor, even if this means that the edges of the piece once it is pin-fitted will not be parallel to the grain. Also check that each piece will be running in the right direction. Cut out the pieces using long-bladed shears.

Write the letter indicating the section on the wrong side of each piece, again using tailor's chalk. Also mark the top end and the direction of the lengthwise grain if it isn't obvious. The centers of the inside and outside backs, the seat, and the front can be marked with pins.

PIN-FITTING

This is the traditional technique used for slipcovers.

Pin-fitting upholstered furniture

The technique works best on upholstered furniture. Chairs and sofas are pin-fitted in the same way—the main difference is the need to join fabric widths for sofas (see above).

2 Usually the inside back and outside back are pinned first, followed by the seat, inside arm, and outside arm if it's an armchair or sofa (and the front arm if the style dictates), then the front, and finally, if it's a wing chair, the inside wing and outside wing. A boxing strip (a narrow rectangular strip of fabric running between two fabric pieces that are roughly parallel) or a gusset (a fairly small, irregularly shaped piece of fabric between two fabric pieces) is dealt with when the adjacent pieces are pin-fitted. Seat and back cushions are covered separately.

1 The fabric rectangles are draped over the chair or sofa, one by one, with the centers matching, and pinned to the upholstery with T-pins inserted at right angles. If the slipcover is snug-fitting, the fabric should be pin-fitted right side up, because chairs and sofas are not precisely symmetrical. However, if the cover is quite loose, you can get away with pin-fitting it wrong side up, which is quicker. (Pattern matching and motif positioning, however, are easier when the fabric is right side up.)

3 As you add fabric pieces, pin them together along the seams, so that they are snug but not tight. Put the pins in nose to tail at this stage, for the most accurate fit. Shaping (see page 108) is done as you go, as is trimming the excess seam allowances to 1 in (2.5cm). To make the fabric go around corners, you will have to clip into the seam allowance at some corners (see page 105), but avoid clipping too deeply at this stage; you can always clip a bit farther later, but you can't put it back if you cut too far! Tuck-ins should also be pinned now (see page 114).

4 Mark each seamline on the wrong side. If the fabric is wrong side up, you simply draw along the pinned lines on the outside using tailor's chalk. If it is right side up, you'll need to open out each seam you've pinned together so that you can mark the seamline along the pins on the wrong side of both pieces.

5 Remove the T-pins and take the cover off the chair. Draw straighter seamlines using a straightedge and tailor's chalk, taking care not to make the cover any tighter. Trim the seam allowances to ⅝ in (1.5cm).

6 If the cover has been pinned with right sides together, piping (see page 120) should now be inserted into the seams (if you are using it). You may wish to put in some crosswise pins between the nose-to-tail ones. The cover is now ready to be stitched.

7 If the pieces are pinned with wrong sides together, they need to be repinned with right sides together before they can be stitched. Before unpinning the pieces, you may find it useful to cut single, double, or triple V-shaped balance marks into both seam allowances simultaneously for each seam. The balance marks, which should be at 2 in (5cm) intervals, can then be matched when repinning. Don't unpin the whole cover at once—unpin and repin pieces as you go, with right sides together. Use the marked lines (and the balance marks, if you have done them) as guides, and insert piping (see page 120) in the seams if you are using it.

RIGHT On this slipcover, the area between the inside and outside backs has been filled by a gusset. To make a similar armchair cover, see pages 26–29.

8 Stitch the seams, press them, and finish the seam allowances (see page 104). If there is a skirt, it is assembled, the pleats are formed (see page 108), and then the skirt is stitched to the rest of the cover. If there is no skirt, the lower edge of the cover is usually hemmed (see page 107), and possibly also faced to hold it in place (see page 114). The zipper or alternative closure, if used, is installed last (see page 112).

Pin-fitting other chairs

You can use pin-fitting on chairs that are not upholstered, though it is more difficult because you cannot anchor the fabric pieces to the chair with T-pins. Nevertheless, you can pin the pieces to each other in the same way, fitting and trimming as you go.

If you make a "sleeve" from some scrap fabric to fit over the back of the chair, this will give you something to which you can pin the first pieces. (The technique for making a sleeve can also be used to make a short cover for the top part of a chair back.)

Making a "sleeve"

1 To make a scrap-fabric "sleeve" to use in pin-fitting another cover, cut two rectangles that are large enough to cover part of the chair back. Placing one at the front and one at the back, pin them together around the top and side edges of the chair back, allowing for a ⅝ in (1.5cm) seam. If the top is fairly straight, either because the chair back is straight or because the vertical posts project only a little above the horizontal rails, you can make this piece by simply folding one piece of fabric in half. If the posts project well above the top of the back rails, simply leave gaps in the top seam. Stitch the seam. Turn the sleeve right side out and slip it over the chair back.

2 To use this technique to make a proper cover for the top part of a chair back, complete step 1, and then, before turning the sleeve right side out, snip off any corners at the top, and clip into the seam allowances on curves. Press under a narrow double hem along the lower edge, and hand sew or machine stitch.

SEAMS

There are probably more seams in a slipcover than in any other home sewing project. Dealing with seams that appear to go off in all directions can seem daunting, but the process becomes much simpler when you break it down into small stages.

BASTING

Whether done by hand or by machine, basting consists of long straight stitches, which are much easier to rip out than regular stitching. It is used to hold fabric layers together temporarily—for example, while you check the fit or shape of a cover, or while you are stitching a seam.

Use basting when you wouldn't be able to remove pins easily prior to stitching (for example, for piping, zippers, or the tops of pleats) or when stitching tricky seams. These include seams you cannot pin or hold easily while stitching, seams involving corners (see page 106), seams in velvet fabric, and seams where one piece is slightly larger than the other and you have to ease in the fullness. Many people prefer to baste all seams before stitching them.

Machine basting is done with a long straight stitch on the sewing machine; hand basting is done as long running stitches. Remove basting that is visible after the seam has been stitched or that stops the seam allowances lying flat.

STITCHING SEAMS

Plain seams are generally used for slipcovers. The stitching does not show on the right side of the fabric.

QUICK RELEASE

To remove machine basting, clip the thread at regular intervals (the distance apart depends on the fabric) and then simply pull on the bobbin thread.

1 Place the fabric pieces with right sides together. The raw edges that are to be seamed should be even. Pin the seam at regular intervals—on curves or areas where you are easing in fullness, the pins will need to be quite close together. Pins are placed nose to tail when slipcovers are being pin-fitted (see page 102) and can be left like this prior to stitching, in which case you must remove each pin as you get to it. Remember to position the pins with the heads at the bottom (with the fabric raw edges on the right) so that they are easy to remove. Pins can be placed at right angles to the seamline to allow you to stitch over them (but only if your sewing machine manual recommends it). You may wish to hand baste the seam (see Basting, above) and then remove the pins before stitching the seam.

2 Set the stitch length to 10–12 stitches per inch (2.5cm). With the raw edges on the right and the bulk of the fabric on the left, stitch the seam at the specified distance from the raw edges. Seam allowances of ⅝ in (1.5cm) are fairly standard and are used in this book, apart from those for closures, which are generally 1 in (2.5cm). Occasionally—for example, when ties are being stitched—seams of ⅜ in (1cm) are used. If there is a stitching guide on your machine, use it to keep the seam an even width. If there isn't a guide, attach a magnetic gauge or a piece of tape to use instead.

3 At each end of the seam, stitch a few stitches in reverse to secure the threads—this is particularly important if you are leaving an opening in a seam. Alternatively, you can secure the threads by tying them: from the wrong side, pull the top thread toward the stitching, and with a pin pull the small loop that is formed. This will bring the other thread through to the wrong side so that you can tie the two threads and then cut off the ends.

MATCHING PATTERNS AT SEAMS

This trick makes accurate pattern matching much easier.

1 Press under the seam allowance on one edge and, with both pieces right side up, lap this seam allowance over the seam allowance of the other piece, so the raw edges are even.

2 Adjust the positions until the pattern matches exactly, and pin the seam in a few places. Flip the top piece over without moving the seam allowance, and then pin the pieces together along the seamline from the wrong side. If you wish, baste them together from the right side, using ladderstitch (page 111).

PRESSING SEAMS

Press straight seams prior to finishing the raw edges, and press curved seams after finishing and clipping them. Try to press as you work. Always press a seam before stitching one that intersects it.

Press the seam flat first, to embed the stitches, and then press it open from the wrong side. If you notice ridged lines forming on the right side as a result, use just the point of the iron or put a press cloth between the iron and the fabric.

FINISHING SEAMS

To stop the raw edges of seams from raveling, they need to be finished in some way. Stitched-and-pinked edges are one option. Make a line of stitching ⅜ in (1cm) from each raw edge, and then cut the raw edge with pinking shears. (Pinking the edges without stitching them is better than nothing but will not really prevent raveling if the cover is laundered.)

Zigzagging the raw edges is another good option. If you are sewing long, straight seams that won't be trimmed, you could do this before stitching them. Otherwise, do it afterward—you may find

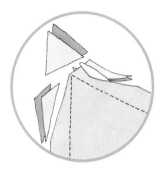

At an outward corner, trim off the point of the seam allowance. If it is a very sharp corner, also trim the seam allowance on either side so that it tapers. At an inward corner, clip into the seam allowance.

For curved seams to lie flat and smooth, you must clip into the seam allowances at regular intervals. Use only the tips of very sharp scissors, and be careful not to cut through the stitching.

ABOVE *Pattern matching at seams is more important on a fabric with a noticeable pattern than on one with a small or random pattern. To make a slipcover similar to this, see pages 18–21, adding scallops to the lower edge (see pages 76–77 and 116).*

TRIMMING, GRADING, AND CLIPPING SEAMS

If a seam is bulky, trimming away about half the seam allowance will help to reduce the bulk.

If a seam is enclosed or forms an edge, the seam allowances should be graded to reduce the bulk. First trim half the seam allowance from both raw edges of the stitched seam, then trim a little more from the seam allowance that will be farthest away from the outside of the cover. If a seam has several layers that will all be turned in one direction rather than pressed open, trim each one a slightly different amount, but avoid trimming too near the seamline, which would weaken the seam.

When a seam crosses another seam, trim away as much as you can of the seam allowances of the seam that was stitched first.

it easier to finish each seam as soon as you have stitched it, rather than completing the whole cover. Use a medium stitch width and a short stitch length. Stitch the edges separately, close to the edge. Make sure that the seam allowances do not pucker up.

One other alternative is to coat the raw edges with liquid fray preventer, which dries invisibly.

If you have an overlock machine, or serger, the seams are stitched, trimmed, and finished all at once.

Occasionally when you are pin-fitting a cover, you may need to clip into a seam allowance before stitching the seam, in order to make the fabric lie flat enough to pin-fit and stitch. In that case, make the clips only ⅜ in (1cm) long; they can be cut slightly closer to the seamline once the seam is actually stitched.

If possible, before clipping into the seam allowance, stitch just inside the seamline through a single layer of fabric, to prevent the clips from tearing beyond the seamline. Known as staystitching, this also helps prevent the fabric from stretching during handling or stitching.

TOPSTITCHING

This form of straight stitching is done from the right side of the fabric and must be very straight. Your stitch guide will be covered up by the material while you are stitching, so to keep the stitching straight, use the presser foot—or a quilting guide-bar attachment or the guide-bar on the walking foot if your machine has either. A strip of tape stuck on the fabric or a line of hand basting would also work.

• For single topstitching, press the seam allowances to one side and then stitch, from the right side, about ⅜ in (1cm) from the seamline through all thicknesses.

• For double topstitching, also known as baseball stitching, press the seam open and then stitch, from the right side, about ⅜ in (1cm) from the seamline, through both thicknesses. Repeat at the other side of the seamline. Start at the same end for both lines of stitching, so that the seam won't pucker.

CORNERS

Slipcovers incorporate many more corners than any other form of home sewing, so it's important to master the technique.

Stitching a corner on two flat pieces

This is the simplest type of corner.

1 Stop stitching when you reach the seamline of the adjacent edge. (To make this easier, you can mark the seamline of the adjacent edge, and use the hand wheel of the machine as you approach the corner.)

2 With the needle in the fabric, raise the presser foot and pivot the fabric 90 degrees to bring the adjacent edge in line with the stitching guide.

3 Lower the presser foot and continue stitching down this seamline.

• To strengthen the seam, use shorter stitches for about 1 in (2.5cm) on each side of the corner.

• On bulky fabric, it's better to stitch a couple of small stitches diagonally across the point, pivoting 45 degrees before and after stitching them.

Stitching a straight edge to an outward corner

Slipcovers incorporate a lot of these, for example when a boxing strip is stitched around the corner of another piece.

1 With the straight piece on top, pin along the seamline as far as the seamline of the adjacent edge. Clip diagonally into the seam allowance of the straight piece exactly even with the corner of the other fabric piece. Be very careful not to clip beyond the seamline—you can always clip a little more later. Ideally, you should

first staystitch (see page 105) just inside the seamline on each side of the corner, to prevent the clip from going over the seamline, but this is not always possible.

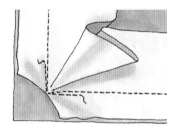

2 Spread out the straight piece so that the clip forms an L-shape. The edge at one side of the clip should be at right angles to the edge at the other side of the clip, and both should be aligned with the edges of the fabric piece beneath.

3 Baste the seam if you wish, and then stitch the seam with the straight, clipped piece still on top. Pivot at the corner, taking care not to catch the excess fabric in the stitching.

Stitching an inward corner to an outward corner

For this, use the same technique as for stitching a straight edge to a corner.

Stitching into a corner

Sometimes a seam joining a straight edge or an inward corner to an outward corner is so inaccessible that pivoting around the corner is difficult. In that situation, you may find it easier to stitch into (but not around) the corner, remove the fabric and cut the threads, then put it back in the machine and stitch into the corner from the adjacent edge. If you do this, you must fasten the threads securely (see page 104) and make sure there is no gap between the stitching lines at the corner.

Leaving seams unstitched at the ends

Because of the corners, seams are not stitched right up to the edge at either end. Instead, start and stop the seam at the seamline of each adjacent seam; for the projects in this book, that will be ⅝ in (1.5cm) from the edge. If you forget, you will need to rip out the ⅝ in (1.5cm) of stitching. (For an edge that will be hemmed, such as the lower edge of a cover, you should stitch right to the edge.)

HEMS

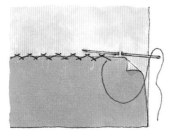

The hems on the covers in this book are generally double hems, made simply by turning under the fabric by the specified amount—often 1 in (2.5cm) in this book—and pressing it, and then turning it under again by the same amount and pressing it once more, then pinning. Finally, the hem is either hand sewn, using a stitch such as catchstitch (shown above) or slipstitch (see page 111), or machine stitched.

On deep hems, hand sewing is preferable but on the relatively shallow hems used in this book—about 1 in (2.5cm) or less—either can be used. Bear in mind, though, that machine stitching will show from the right side (unless your machine has a blindstitch or hemmer foot).
• If you are using bulky fabric, a double hem is not advisable. Instead, zigzag stitch the raw edge and then make just a single hem.

Mitering hem corners

On most slipcovers the hems don't have corners, but if you do make a cover that has hemmed corners, for example when the skirt consists of separate panels at each side, you'll need to miter each one.

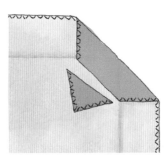

• To miter a corner where two narrow single hems of the same width meet, first press the hems in the usual way and then open out the pressed fold on each hem. Fold the corner in diagonally so that the creases line up. Trim off the corner, ¼ in (5mm) outside the diagonal fold, to reduce bulk. Refold the hems and slipstitch the miter (where the two diagonal folds meet).

RISING HEMLINES
For slipcovers that extend to the floor, the hemline should actually be about 1 in (2.5cm) above the floor so that the cover won't gather dust.

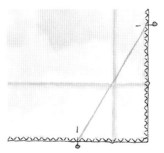

• To miter a corner where two narrow single hems of different sizes meet, open out the fold on one hem and mark with a pin on that edge the point where the other (folded) hem comes to. Fold it again, open out the fold on the other hem, and mark with a pin on that edge the point where the folded hem comes to. Now open out the folds on both hems, and draw a line between the pins. Remove the pins, fold along this line, and trim off the corner, ¼ in (5mm) outside the fold. Refold both hems and slipstitch the miter.
• To miter a corner where two narrow double hems meet, turn under and press the first fold on each side, then turn under and press the second fold on each side (rather than doing both folds on one hem, then both on the other). Open out the second fold but not the first fold on each side, and then follow the above instructions (as though the first fold on each side weren't there).

SEAMS IN BATTING

If you are joining two pieces of batting, simply overlap the edges by the total of the two seam allowances, so the seamlines are aligned, and zigzag stitch them together, then trim the seam allowances. If the batting is very thick, cut off the seam allowances, butt up the edges instead of overlapping them, and then sew them together by hand using catchstitch (see above).

When batting is stitched in a seam with fabric, trim away the batting seam allowance, right up to the stitching line. The stitching will hold it in place.

SHAPING

Where fabric covers a curved area, some method of shaping the fabric is needed, to dispose of excess fullness in a seam. There are several ways of doing this.

DARTS

Most darts are stitched wedges of fabric that are widest at the edge of the fabric and taper to nothing. You may need just one dart or several in a group. Darts are formed on the wrong side of the fabric, but if you are pin-fitting a cover right side out, you can pin it on the right side and then unpin and repin it on the wrong side when you do the same for the seams.

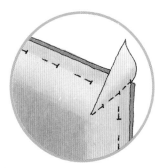

1 With the fabric in position on the chair, pin it so that the fullness is taken up in the dart. (If you will need more than one, start with the central dart.) The fabric edges should be even and the pins in a straight line, tapering to a point. Baste if you wish, removing the pins.

2 Stitch from the wide end of the dart to the point. Be careful to taper gradually—you should be stitching quite close to the fold as you get near the point. At the point, tie the threads rather than attempting to stitch in reverse.

3 If necessary, make other darts of equal size on each side of the first one. Press the dart(s) to one side. Or, if the fabric is bulky, cut along the fold of the dart(s) almost to the point, and press open.

RELEASED TUCKS

These stitched folds are made on the wrong side of the fabric. Technically they are known as released tucks or dart tucks (as distinct from plain tucks, which are purely decorative—see page 122).

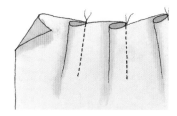

However, in the context of pin-fitting slipcovers, they are often just called tucks. They are made in the same way as darts, but the stitching is parallel to the fold, rather than tapering to a point. Stop stitching at the end (known as the release point) of each tuck.

KNIFE PLEATS AND BOX PLEATS

Pleats are folds of fabric that are not stitched along the length but are held in place only at the top. They can be pressed or left unpressed.

Very small knife pleats (in which the folds all face in the same direction) can be used in the same way as darts (see above) and released tucks (see above), either individually or in groups. Larger knife pleats are generally used in groups rather than individually and can be used all the way around a slipcover skirt.

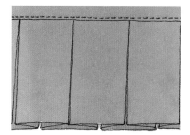

Sometimes a slipcover skirt has box pleats (pairs of knife pleats with the folds facing away from each other).

INVERTED PLEATS

The large pleats known as inverted pleats are pairs of knife pleats with the folds facing each other and meeting in the center of the pleat. They are often used individually at the corners of a table cover or slipcover skirt, or sometimes at center back of the slipcover.

1 Measure the extra fabric allocated to the pleat and, with tailor's chalk, mark a central placement line and two outer fold lines on the wrong side of the fabric. For the projects in this book, 12 in (30cm) of extra fabric is allowed for each pleat, so the outer fold lines will each be 6 in (15cm) away from the placement line. The inner fold lines will be halfway between the outer fold lines and the placement line, so it's not necessary to mark them.

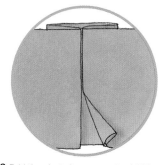

2 Fold the pleat along one outer fold line and bring the fold to the placement line. Pin at the top. Repeat for the other fold, which faces the first one. Baste across the top of the pleat.

3 If the pleat is to be pressed, pin along the length of the folds through all three thicknesses. Hand baste along the length of both folds, removing the pins. Using a press cloth, press the pleats from the right side and then from the wrong side. Remove the lengthwise basting. If the pleat is to be unpressed, skip this step.

● It's preferable to hem the fabric before making pleats, but if the skirt needs to be pinned to the cover before you can adjust the length, you'll probably find it easier to hem the skirt after making them. While a cover is on a chair and you are marking the hemline at the lower edge, hold the pleats closed with masking tape. After taking the cover off the chair, remove the tape and open out the pleat at the lower edge while you press and sew the hem. Finally, re-press the folds of the pleat.

● Sometimes the upper part of an inverted pleat is topstitched through all thicknesses. If you don't want the center of the topstitched part to open at all, stitch first along the seamline, right sides together, as far as the release point; press. Now, from the right side, starting in the center of the pleat at the release point, stitch outward at a right angle to the fold for about ⅜ in (1cm), then pivot and stitch toward the top of the pleat. Starting again in the center at the release point, stitch outward in the opposite direction for ⅜ in (1cm) before pivoting and stitching to the top along that side. Tie the threads on the wrong side.

ABOVE *Details such as pleats and ties at the back are ideal for dining chairs. To make this chair cover, follow the instructions on pages 52–55. For the table cover, make the cover on pages 40–41, but omit the binding and ties, and simply hem the edges.*

Separate pleat underlays

The inside of an inverted pleat is known as the underlay. In its simplest form, the pleat and its underlay are all the same piece of fabric. But if you are incorporating ties to hold the pleat closed, these should be inserted in seams joining a separate underlay to the main fabric. Another reason for having a separate underlay is to allow it to be cut from a contrasting fabric. Depending on the desired effect, the underlay seams can run along either the outer folds of the pleat or the inner ones.

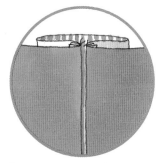

• For seams on the outer folds, the underlay width should be twice the desired pleat width, plus 1¼ in (3cm) for seam allowances. The main fabric should have nothing added to the width apart from ⅝ in (1.5cm) for a seam allowance to the main fabric on the left side of the pleat, and the same to the main fabric on the right.

• For seams on the inner folds, the underlay width should be the desired pleat width, plus 1¼ in (3cm) for seam allowances. Half that amount should be added to the main fabric on the left of the pleat, and half to the main fabric on the right.

Whichever type of separate underlay you have, the main fabric and separate underlays will alternate on a slipcover skirt, and you need to measure carefully when joining them.

Once you have completed the pleats and pressed the hem, clip into the seam allowances of each underlay just above the stitched edge of the hem. Trim close to the seamline beneath the clip, to make the seam less bulky. Now sew the hem and re-press the folds of the pleat.

GATHERS

These are tiny, soft folds of fabric, which can be almost unnoticeable or quite large, depending on the amount of fullness to accommodate.

1 Hand or machine baste two rows of stitching inside the seamline, leaving ends at least 4 in (10cm) long.

2 Secure the bobbin threads (or both threads if you have used hand basting) at one end by wrapping them in a figure-of-eight around a pin. At the other end, pull the two bobbin threads (or both threads if hand-basted) to form tiny, soft folds in the fabric.

3 Continue pulling up the gathers until the edge of the fabric is the right length, spreading out the gathers evenly.

4 When you stitch a seam with gathered fabric, stitch with the gathered piece on top so that you can keep the gathers straight and even.

CUTAWAY AREAS

Occasionally, slipcovers have to be cut and shaped around chair arms and legs. The easiest way of finishing the edges of these cutaway areas is with a facing (a separate piece of fabric that is the same shape as the edge it is stitched to).

1 With tailor's chalk, mark on the right side where the finished edge of the cutaway area around the arm or leg should be; this will be the seamline. Cut away the fabric to leave a ⅜ in (1cm) seam allowance.

2 From scrap fabric, cut a facing to fit the cutaway area. Each side of the facing should be about 1¼ in (3cm) wide. Zigzag stitch the outer edges to finish them.

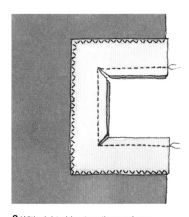

3 With right sides together and raw edges even, pin the facing to the cutaway area around all three sides. Stitch a ⅜ in (1cm) seam, along the inner edges, pivoting at the corners. Clip into the seam allowance diagonally at each corner, taking care not to clip through the stitching. Grade the seam.

4 Fold the facing to the wrong side of the cutaway area, and press. Slipstitch it in place around the edge.

• The instructions above are for a rectangular cutaway area, but much the same technique can be used for a curved one. Instead of pivoting at corners and then clipping into them, stitch the seam as one curve and then clip into the seam allowance on the curve.

SECURING

Many covers—such as slipcovers for chairs that are wider at the top than at the bottom—need some sort of closure to allow them to be put onto the item that they are covering. There are also a couple of methods to stop covers from slipping off once they are in place.

SLIPSTITCHED CLOSURES

When an opening is left in a cover so that the cover can be turned right side out, the opening is slipstitched, which, unlike topstitching, does not show. Slipstitching is also often used to close openings in cushion covers after the cushion form has been slipped inside. To remove the cover for laundering, the slipstitching is cut, and then redone when the cushion form has been put back in the clean cover.

Even if most of one side has to be left open for a cushion to be inserted, the cushion will have a more professional finish if the machine-stitched seam runs around both corners. Starting the opening at each corner does not give as crisp a look or as durable a finish.

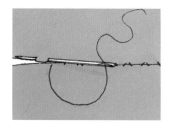

To sew together the two folded edges of an opening, start at the right and hide the knot in one folded edge, bringing the needle out through the fold. Insert it into the other folded edge 1/16 in (1–2mm) to the left, slip the needle through the fold, and bring it out 1/4 in (5mm) to the left. Repeat on the opposite folded edge, and continue in the same way. The minute stitches make the sewing almost invisible.

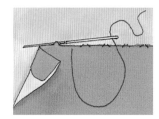

• Slipstitch can also be used to sew a folded edge to a flat piece, for example in hand sewing a hem. Instead of slipping the needle through a second fold, pick up a few threads on the flat piece. When the stitches within the fold are 3/4 in (2cm) long, the stitch is known as ladderstitch; this is used as a basting stitch when matching patterns in seams (see page 104).

OVERLAP CLOSURES

Also known as envelope closures, these are quick and easy to make, and so are often used at the back of pillow and cushion covers. Unless supplied with buttons or snaps, these closures can gape open if the pillow or cushion is quite large, preventing the front from fitting tightly.

1 Cut the back to the same length as the front, and to a width equal to the width of the front plus 3 1/2 in (8.5cm). Cut the back in half lengthwise (from top to bottom). Turn under and press a double 1/4 in (5mm) hem on the inner edge of each piece. Pin and topstitch.

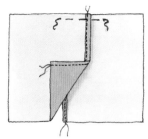

2 With right sides up, lap the hemmed edge of one side over the other by about 2 1/2 in (6.5cm), so the width is the same as that of the front. Baste at the top and bottom just inside the seamline. Now treat the back as one piece.

BUTTON CLOSURES

The outside back of a slipcover can be given an overlap closure (see above), with buttonholes made in the overlap and buttons sewn to the underlap. To make buttonholes, follow the directions in your sewing machine manual.

Covered buttons

For a smart look, use covered buttons on the slipcover. On chairs arranged around a dining table, the lines of buttons running down the chair backs look especially striking, and they also look good running alongside pleats (in which case they are not functional but merely decorative).

1 Covered buttons are made using covered-button kits. For each button, cut a fabric circle with a diameter about 5/8 in (1.5cm) larger than that of the button (or the size specified in the kit). Hand baste around the outer edge of the circle, leaving the ends of the thread long.

2 Place the button form upside down on the wrong side of the circle. Pull the thread while holding the other end, so that the edge of the fabric circle curls up around the button form. Knot the threads, and cut off the ends. Stretch the fabric over opposite sides until it catches on the hooks inside the button form. Repeat all around the button form.

3 Smooth out any bumps in the fabric, and then press the back plate into the back of the button form.

GROMMETS

Cord threaded through a line of large grommets on each side of an opening or pleat looks very stylish on a variety of covers. You will need a kit to make the grommets. The methods vary from kit to kit, but often they involve first making a hole in the fabric with sharp, pointy scissors, inserting the pointed end of the tool in the hole, placing the grommet on the point, and clamping the tool together, like pliers. This flattens the edges of the grommet over the hole, covering up any raw fabric edges.

ZIPPERS

These are often used in both slipcovers and cushion covers. Although they take a little while to install, they are unobtrusive and very practical. Use an upholstery zipper, as these are longer and stronger than dressmaker's zippers.

Installing a zipper in a slipcover

On a chair, a zipper is conventionally installed in the back right-hand seam, and on a sofa in both back seams. They are put in slipcovers after everything else—including the piping, skirt, and hem—has been completed. The zipper needs to be about 2–4 in (5–10cm) shorter than the seam into which it will be installed, because it does not go all the way to the top. It opens from the bottom up. These instructions are for a zipper at the back right-hand side; for the other side, reverse "left" and "right."

1 Trim the seam allowance to 1 in (2.5cm). Zigzag the raw edges of the seam. With the pull tab of the closed zipper ⅝ in (1.5cm) from the bottom edge, mark with a pin where the zipper stop will be at the other end. Pin and stitch a 1 in (2.5cm) wide seam from the top down to the pin. Press under the seam allowances for the remainder of the seam.

2 With the cover right side out, open out the right-hand seam allowance. Position the open zipper face down on it, with the teeth just next to the seamline. (If you have piped the slipcover, the piping should have been basted to this side of the seam; the zipper teeth should just cover the edge of the piping.) Pin and baste the tape at the left to the seam allowance. At the bottom of the cover, turn up the end of the zipper tape, and fold in the fabric seam allowance diagonally, pinning and basting them in place.

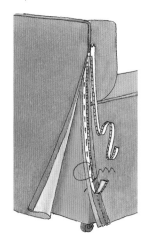

3 With the zipper foot on the machine, stitch to the left of the teeth, very close to them. If the cover has a skirt with a pleat at the opening, stop the stitching when you get to the skirt, and then start stitching again at the top of the skirt on the pleat underlay (the lower layer).

4 Turn over the zipper, turning under the seam allowance. Close the zipper and lap

the pressed edge of the other side of the opening over the zipper to meet the first edge. At the bottom of the cover, turn under the end of the zipper tape, and fold in the fabric seam allowance diagonally, pinning and basting them in place.

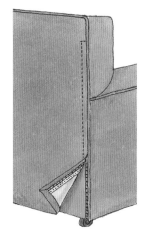

5 With the zipper foot on the machine, begin topstitching at the bottom of the zipper (which is near the top of the seam), at the seamline. Stitch across the lapped seam, pivot, and then stitch down that side. Again, if there is a skirt with a pleat, break the stitching at the skirt so that you can stitch through the underlay.

Installing a zipper in a box cushion cover

On a box cushion the zipper is installed into two "zipper strips," which replace the boxing strip at the back. On a square or rectangular cushion, a T-cushion, or an L-shaped cushion, the zipper should extend about 2 in (5cm) around each back corner. However, if the sides will be visible, it should not extend around the corners. And if the cushion is a spring cushion that must not be folded, it should extend around each back corner by about 4 in (10cm).

The width of each of the two zipper strips should be half the thickness of the cushion, plus 1⅝ in (4cm). Their length should be the length of the zipper, plus 2 in (5cm).

1 With right sides together, pin the two zipper strips together along the inner long edges with a 1 in (2.5cm) seam. Stitch the seam at each end for 1 in (2.5cm), backstitching and then machine basting in between. The machine-basted portion should be the length of the zipper from just outside the top and bottom stops. Zigzag the edges of the seam allowances and press the seam open.

2 On the wrong side of the fabric, lay the closed zipper, face down, along the seamline of the basted portion. Hand baste in place down both sides of the zipper and across the top and bottom, just outside the zipper stops.

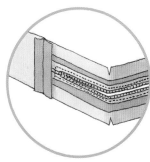

3 With the zipper foot on the machine, topstitch the zipper about ¼ in (5mm) from the edge of the opening. If the fabric does not have a tendency to creep, you can start at one end and stitch down one side, across the bottom, up the other side, and across the other end. Be careful to stitch outside the zipper stops (use your basting as a guide). Tie the threads on the wrong side. If the fabric does tend to creep, you'll

have to stitch across one end and down one side, then begin again at the end you started at and stitch down the other side in the same direction as for the first side, then across the other end. Remove the basting and open the zipper before stitching the zipper strips to the boxing strip and the top and bottom of the cushion cover.

VELCRO CLOSURES

Sew-on Velcro tape can be used instead of a zipper on a chair or sofa slipcover or as a cushion closure. Two interlocking strips, one with tiny hooks and the other with tiny soft loops, are pressed together to close the opening and are pulled apart to open it. Velcro closures have to be set into a lapped opening, for which you'll need to add ¾ in (2cm) to the dimensions of the fabric at each side of the opening.

Applying Velcro tape

1 Cut the Velcro to ½ in (1.2cm) longer than the opening if it is in a slipcover, or 1 in (2.5cm) longer if it is in a cushion. Trim the seam allowance to ¾ in (2cm). Zigzag the raw edges of the seam. Pin and stitch a ¾ in (2cm) seam for about 2 in (5cm) above the opening if in a slipcover, or at both ends of the opening if in a cushion cover. Press under the seam allowances for the remainder of the seam.

2 Trim the seam allowance that will form the overlap to ½ in (1.2cm). If you have piped the slipcover, this is the side that should have the piping. Separate the tape. Pin or baste the hook strip along the fold of this seam allowance, hook side up, with the end extending beyond the top of the slipcover opening by ½ in (1.2cm), or each end extending beyond the cushion cover opening by that amount. The tape will also extend beyond the side edge of the seam allowance. If the edge is piped, pin or baste the tape on top of the piping seam allowance.

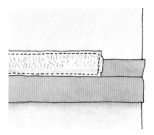

3 Stitch along both long edges and both ends, through the seam allowance and the main fabric. If the slipcover has a skirt with a pleat at the opening, stop stitching when you reach the skirt, then begin again at the top of the skirt so that you can stitch through the pleat underlay.

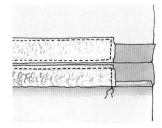

4 Pin the loop strip to the wrong side of the other seam allowance so that the tape overlaps the seam allowance by only ⅛ in (3mm). The wrong side of the tape should be against the wrong side of the seam allowance. As before, each end should extend beyond the opening by ½ in (1.2cm). Stitch along the long edge through the tape and seam allowances only.

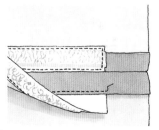

5 Turn the loop strip to the right side of the seam allowance; the loop side of the tape should now be on top. Stitch along the other long edge and both ends, again stitching through the tape and seam allowance only.

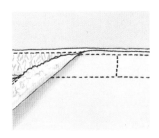

6 Turn the cover right side out, and place the hook strip over the loop strip.

• Another type of Velcro can be used at the lower edge of a slipcover to hold it in place—see page 115.

OTHER TAPE CLOSURES

Snap tape (with regularly spaced balls on one strip and sockets on the other) and hook-and-eye tape (with regularly spaced hooks on one strip and eyes on the other) are applied in the same way as Velcro.

TIES

Pairs of ties are often used to hold pleats or pieces of fabric together, or to secure cushions to chairs. There are two principal ways of making them.

• With one method, no stitching is visible. Cut the fabric to twice the width you require, plus ¾ in (2cm), and fold each fabric piece in half lengthwise, with right sides together. Pin and stitch a ⅜ in (1cm) seam down the long edge and across one end, and then turn the tie right side out. (Placing the stitched end on the blunt end of a skewer or knitting needle and pulling the tie down over it makes this easier.) If both ends of the tie will show, turn in the raw edges at the end and slipstitch the opening closed. If, however, one end will be inserted in a seam, you could just zigzag the end, as it will not be visible.

• The other method can be used for very narrow ties, which are tricky to turn right side out if stitched using the previous method—but the stitching shows on the right side. Cut fabric to twice the width you require, plus ½ in (1cm). Turn under and press ¼ in (5mm) on each long edge and one or both ends (depending on whether both ends will be visible or not). Fold the strip in half lengthwise, and stitch along the turned-under edges.

Inserting ties in a seam

Ties can simply be sewn onto fabric, but they will be much stronger if they are inserted in a seam. Sandwich the tie between the two layers, with the end even with the raw edges of the seam, and stitch through the tie as you stitch the seam. If the seam is already stitched—for example, if you cannot judge the positions of the ties until the cover has been stitched—rip out the portion of the seam where the tie is to be, insert the end of the tie, and restitch the seam.

BIG TIES

Most ties used in slipcovers are relatively narrow, but big bold ties, which are made and inserted in seams in the same way as narrow ones, can look very striking. For example, you could make a slipcover with a very loose outside back, then insert large ties in the seams at the sides, and either loop them together or tie them into big floppy bows at the back.

TUCK-INS

Slipcovers for upholstered chairs and sofas are always made with tuck-ins, which hold crucial parts of the slipcover in place while allowing some movement of the cover in use. Tuck-ins are curved pockets of fabric that are pushed into the crevices around the seat, and also between the arms and back, and between a wing chair's wings and back.

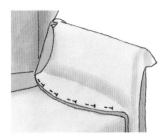

Tuck-ins are constructed by allowing enough extra fabric on adjacent fabric pieces, and then pinning the two pieces together and trimming them to form a curved pocket. The depth of tuck-ins varies according to the depth of the crevice. Often the crevices around the seat are the deepest. A tuck-in of 3–6 in (7.5–15cm) is standard, so the tuck-in allowances given for each project in this book allow 6 in (15cm)—you can reduce them if necessary. Taper the tuck-in from the maximum depth in the center to only the seam allowance at the edges.

FACINGS

These can make all the difference to the look of a slipcover. They are basically just flaps that are sewn to each side at the lower edge of the cover to hold it in place on the underside. They require a ⅝ in (1.5cm) seam allowance rather than a 2 in (5cm) allowance for a double hem along the lower edge.

1 From scrap fabric, cut a facing for each side of the chair or sofa at the lower edge. Each should be 3¾ in (9.5cm) wide,

LEFT *Slipcovers on upholstered chairs are held in place by invisible "tuck-ins" between the seat, arms, and back. This cover is made like the sofa cover on pages 22–25, but each side boxing strip is made up of two pieces—top and front.*

TACKING STRIPS

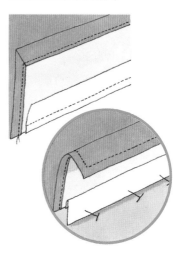

and as long as the distance between the legs plus 1¼ in (3cm). Turn under, press, and stitch ⅝ in (1.5cm) on one long edge and both ends of each facing.

2 Cut a length of sew-and-stick Velcro to fit each facing. Separate the strips, and stitch one strip to the wrong side of each facing, near the long hemmed edge.

3 With right sides together and raw edges even, pin the unfinished raw edge of each facing to the lower edge of the cover between the legs. If the lower edge is piped, just pin the facing over it. Stitch ⅝ in (1.5cm) from the raw edges all the way around, even between the facings.

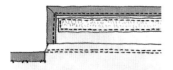

4 Press the facings and seam allowances away from the cover; topstitch the facing to the seam allowance. Known as understitching, this will prevent the facing from rolling to the outside. Clip into the seam allowance alongside each facing. Press under ¼ in (5mm) and then ⅜ in (1cm) on the unfaced edges between the clips, and hand sew on the wrong side.

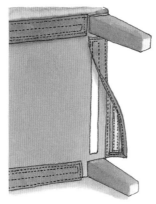

5 Stick the other strips of Velcro to the underside of the chair or sofa, in positions corresponding to the strips on the facings. Press the Velcro strips together to hold the slipcover in place.

• If you don't want to stick Velcro to the underside of your chair, you can turn the facings into casings for a "drawstring." On each facing, turn under and press a double ¾ in (2cm) hem, and stitch along the turned-under edge. Using a large, blunt needle or a safety pin, thread a length of cord or narrow tape through the casings. Put the cover on the chair and tie the drawstring securely.

• Facings are also used for constructing shaped edges (see page 116) and for neatening cutaway areas (see page 110).

A slipcover with a skirt can be secured in a similar way to facings. Cut four strips of scrap fabric about 3½ in (9cm) wide and a length equal to the width of each side of the skirt. After pinning the top edge of the skirt to the lower edge of the cover with right sides together and raw edges even, pin the tacking strips on top. Stitch the seam through all layers.

Put the cover on the chair or sofa, lift the skirt, and pin the tacking strips to the chair or sofa with T-pins. These will be covered by the skirt.

TWIST PINS

Just as T-pins are used here to discreetly secure the cover, so twist pins can be employed at strategic points to prevent part of a slipcover from sagging. They are easy to remove when you want to take off the cover.

DECORATIVE ADDITIONS

There are lots of ways to make covers look stylish, from the very subtle to the completely over the top. Many of these additions also have a practical function.

SHAPED EDGES

Instead of a straight, hemmed edge on an overlap closure at the back of a slipcover, or on the lower edge of a slipcover, seat cover, table cover, or bedcover, you could use a facing to make a scalloped, zigzag, or castellated edge.

1 When cutting out the fabric that will have the shaped edge, allow extra beyond the hemline, to form a facing a bit deeper than the shaped outline. Press under ¼ in (5mm) along the edge; stitch. Turn the facing to the outside (right sides together) along the hemline.

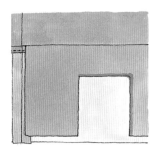

2 Measure the length of the edge, and work out the size and number of shapes you will need to fill it exactly. (For scallops, see page 76.) Make a cardboard template of the shape. Starting at a back seam, place it ¼ in (5mm) away from the folded edge of the facing, and draw around the shape with a fabric marker. Move the template along the facing and repeat the process until the shapes extend around the whole skirt. You may need to cheat a little on the size of the final shapes to fit them all in, but if you do this at the back it won't show.

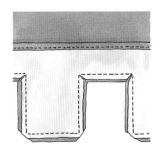

3 Pin and stitch along the marked outline through both layers, pivoting where the design dictates. Cut ¼ in (5mm) outside the stitching line. Grade the seam allowance, snip off the points of outward corners, clip into curves, and clip into any inward corners, being careful to stay within the seam allowance and not cut through the stitching. Turn the facing to the inside, and press. Slipstitch the edge of the facing in place on the wrong side.

BORDERS

These contrasting bands of fabric look chic on the lower edge of a slipcover for a chair or sofa, or on a table or bed cover.

1 Cut a strip of contrasting fabric to the desired width, plus 1¼ in (3cm), and to the same length as the edge to be bordered. Press under ⅝ in (1.5cm) on one long edge of the strip. Pin the other long edge to the edge of the cover, with the right side of the border facing the *wrong* side of the fabric. Stitch a ⅝ in (1.5cm) seam. Grade the seam allowance.

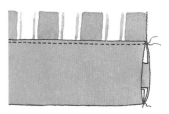

2 Press the border away from the cover, and then to the right side of the cover, with the seamline running along the bottom. Pin and then topstitch along the folded edge at the top of the border.

TRIMMINGS

A look around a good notions department or store will undoubtedly provide inspiration for ways to spice up your slipcovers. An astonishing assortment of gorgeous fringes, ribbon, braids, cords, giant rickrack, and other trimmings is available today. Some are so attractive that you may be inspired to plan a slipcover around them.

Most of these trimmings are topstitched or hand sewn to the right side of the cover, though some, like picot edging, are inserted into the seam in the same way as piping (see page 120).

Ideally, the trimmings should be applied before adjacent seams are stitched, so that the ends can be caught in those seams. If this is not possible, turn under the ends when you sew them on. Where two ends meet, turn under only one end and lap it over the other, in an inconspicuous position.

● In addition to serving a functional purpose (see page 111), buttons can look decorative sewn in lines at either side of a pleat or along a hemmed edge. To make covered buttons, see page 111.

BIAS BINDING

This is used both for binding edges (see page 118) and for piping (see page 120). Although you can use purchased bias binding for either, custom bias binding is preferable because it allows you to use a fabric of the same weight as your main fabric (or, obviously, the same fabric). It will also be exactly the right width. So, even though purchased bias binding is specified in the projects in this book in which the binding is not in the slipcover fabric, making your own would be better.

Making small amounts of bias binding

The simplest method, this is really only practical for small amounts because of the number of individual seams to stitch.

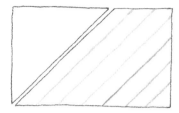

1 Fold over a corner of the fabric so that the lengthwise and crosswise grains match. The diagonal fold line is the true bias. Press along this fold. Now draw lines parallel to the fold—the distance between them should be the desired width of the binding. Cut out the strips.

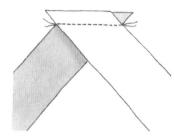

2 With right sides together, pin and stitch the strips together at right angles with diagonal ¼ in (5mm) seams (i.e., on the straight grain). All the seams should slant in the same direction. The side edges of the two strips should meet at each end of the seamline, not at the raw edges of the ends. Trim off the points extending beyond the edges. Press the seams open.

Making large amounts of bias binding

Some slipcovers, such as those for sofas, will require a lot of piping, so it's worth mastering this "continuous strip" method, as it will save a great deal of time.

1 From the fabric, cut a rectangle that is more than twice as long as it is wide. Fold each end on the true bias (see step 1 above). Press and then cut along these lines. (Save the triangles to make separate strips of binding if you wish.)

ABOVE A contrasting trim, such as this red bias binding, can transform a slipcover. The seat and arms of this cover are made in the same way as on pages 18–21, the back as on pages 30–33, and the pleat as on pages 52–55 (using bias binding rather than fabric for the ties). For this scalloped edge, a facing isn't necessary—simply cut 4 in (10cm) semicircles around the lower edge and then bind the raw edge (see page 118).

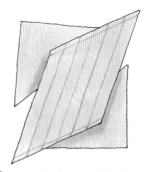

2 Draw cutting lines parallel to the raw slanting ends—the distance between them should be the desired width of the binding. Now draw a seamline ¼ in (5mm) from each long edge.

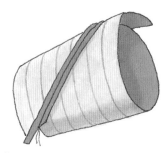

3 Fold the fabric as shown, so the corner of one raw slanting end is even with the first cutting line. Pin the slanting ends together along the seamline. The cutting lines should match all the way across, and there should be one strip overhanging at each end of the resulting tube. Stitch along the pinned seamline and press the seam open.

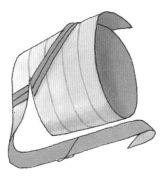

4 Now carefully cut in one continuous line along the cutting line that spirals all the way around the tube.

FABRIC YIELDS

About 1 yd (91cm) of 54 in (137cm) wide fabric will yield approximately 20 yd (18m) of 2 in (5cm) wide bias binding.

BINDING AN EDGE

Binding is a practical way of finishing raw edges, and if you use contrasting binding it can also look very decorative. You can use bias binding you have made yourself (see pages 116–118) or purchased bias binding. For straight edges, the binding can be cut on the straight grain (either lengthwise or crosswise), but for curved edges, bias binding is essential. Whether you want to bind one layer or more than one, the techniques are the same.

Remember that if you will be binding an edge, you should not add a seam allowance to the fabric dimensions when measuring and cutting out. If there already is a seam or hem allowance, trim this off.

Two-stage method

With this method the stitching attaching the binding is not noticeable.

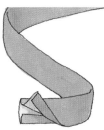

1 If you are making your own bias binding, cut the bias strip to twice the desired finished width, plus ¾ in (2cm). Press under ¼ in (5mm) on both long raw edges. Now fold the binding lengthwise, so the fold is very slightly off-center; press. If you are using purchased bias binding, some or all of these folds will already have been done.

2 Open out the binding and pin the narrower side to the edge of the main fabric, with right sides together and raw edges even. Stitch along the fold line.

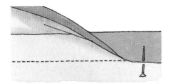

3 When this is complete, bring the binding over to the wrong side of the main fabric, and pin the other folded edge over the stitching. Now either slipstitch from the wrong side or stitch in the ditch (machine stitch in the groove just alongside the binding) from the right side.

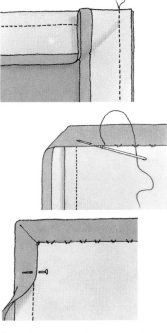

4 To miter an outward corner, stop the stitching in step 2 when you get to the stitching line of the adjacent edge. Backstitch to fasten the thread, and remove the fabric from the machine. Fold the binding so that the edge is even with that of the adjacent edge, and a diagonal fold has formed. Pin and resume stitching along the fold line down the new edge, starting at the upper edge. To stitch the other edge of the binding on the wrong side (step 3), fold the binding into a miter at the corner, and turn the binding to the wrong side over the raw edges, forming another miter in the opposite direction on the wrong side.

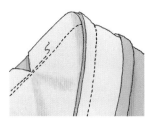

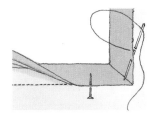

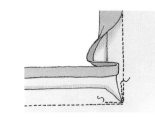

5 To miter an inward corner, reinforce the corner before step 2 by stitching along the fold line for a short distance at each side. Now clip into the fabric seam allowance at the corner. When stitching in step 2, open out the fabric corner so that the edges are in a straight line, and pin it to the binding from the fabric side. Stitch from the fabric side. After you have completed step 2, press the binding away from the fabric on both edges, forming a miter at the corner on the right side. Pull this through the clip to the wrong side. Fold the binding over the edges, forming a miter in the opposite direction at the corner on the wrong side. Complete step 3, slipstitching the miter.

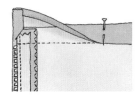

6 To end binding at a finished edge, cut the binding ¼ in (5mm) beyond the edge. Trim the fabric seam allowance diagonally at the corner. Turn under the end of the binding so the fold is even with the finished edge, and finish stitching.

7 To join the binding ends, stitch the same diagonal seam as when joining bias strips to make bias binding (see above).

One-stage method

With this method the stitching is visible, but it is quicker than the two-stage method.

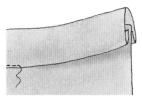

1 If you are making your own bias binding, cut and fold the binding as for the two-stage method, step 1. Slip the folded binding over the fabric edge to encase it, with the wider side of the binding on the wrong side of the fabric. Topstitch close to the edge from the right side.

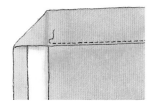

2 To miter an outward corner, stitch as far as the edge, and remove the cover from the machine. Fold the binding diagonally into a miter on both the right and wrong sides. Now resume stitching along the new fold line.

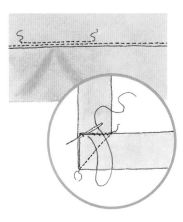

3 To miter an inward corner, reinforce and clip into the corner as for the two-stage method, step 5. Stop stitching at the point of the corner, and pivot as you open out the corner so the edges are in a straight line. Continue stitching down the new edge. When it is finished, fold the binding at the corner to create a miter on the right side. On the wrong side, fold the binding as shown, press, machine stitch the miter, and slipstitch the corner.

4 To end binding at a finished edge, simply turn under ¼ in (5mm) at the end so that it is even with the finished edge, and complete the stitching.

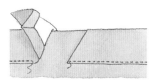

5 To join the ends of the binding, cut the ends diagonally (i.e., on the straight grain), and lap one end over the other, turning under ½ in (1cm) on the overlapping end. Complete the stitching, and slipstitch the overlapped end along the turned-under edge if you wish.

PIPING

Although piping is technically a folded strip of bias binding inserted into a seam, it usually has cording inside it. When the cording is quite thick, the piping is often called welting. Piping the seams of a slipcover adds definition and a professional finish, and it also makes the seams last longer.

When a slipcover is piped, the piping is usually inserted in all the principal exposed seams. With any piping, but especially when it is in a contrasting fabric, piping lines must be very straight.

The cording used inside piping comes in various widths; ¼ in (5mm) is used in the projects in this book, but on a delicate item you could choose ⅛ in (3mm) piping, and on a robust, large-scale piece of furniture you might prefer ½ in (1.2cm). Be sure the cording is preshrunk before you use it (see page 99).

Piping a seam

1 Decide on the width of bias binding you will need to cover your piping cord. In this book we have specified 2 in (5cm) bias binding for the ¼ in (5mm) cording. The easiest way to check the width is to wrap some fabric around the cording, pin it and measure the distance, and then add 1¼ in (3cm) for seam allowances. Also decide the approximate length you need. Make enough bias binding of the right width (see pages 116–117).

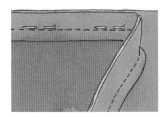

2 Wrap the bias binding around the cording, right side out and with the raw edges even, and pin. With the piping foot or zipper foot on the machine, machine

baste quite close to the cord. (If the basting is too close, however, there is a risk that it will show on the finished cover.)

3 Pin the piping to the right side of one piece of fabric, with the raw edges facing outward. Start in an inconspicuous place, ideally away from a corner and on a straight seam. If the end will be visible on the finished cover, finish it as explained in step 6. Otherwise, leave the first 2 in (5cm) unbasted, so the end can be joined later, as in step 5. The seam allowances of the piping and the cover should be the same so that the raw edges will be even. The basting on the piping should be positioned slightly inside the seamline, so that when the seam is finally stitched (see step 7), it will be tight against the piping, and the basting will not show.

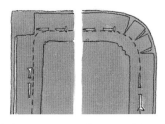

4 Clip into the seam allowances of the piping at corners and on curves. With the piping foot or zipper foot on the machine, machine baste along the previous basting line, starting about ⅝ in (1.5cm) in from the end.

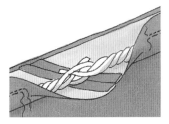

5 To join ends (preferably on an inconspicuous straight edge), stop stitching the piping to the fabric about 2 in (5cm) before the end of the piping. Remove some of the basting at one end of

RIGHT *A ruffle around the lower edge is the finishing touch to this striped slipcover. For a similar cover, follow the instructions on pages 18–21, attaching a ruffle to the lower edge (see page 121).*

the piping and pull back the bias binding. Either trim the cording until the ends butt up, or unravel the cording, trim the strands to different lengths, and intertwine them. Turn under ¼ in (5mm) on one end of the binding, and lap it over the other end as you wrap it around the cording. Restitch the basting on the piping, and continue basting the piping to the cover.

6 To finish the end of piping at an opening, reduce bulk by cutting the cording ¾ in (2cm) before the end. Cut the bias binding ⅜ in (1cm) *beyond* the end. Turn under fabric even with the end and finish basting the piping.

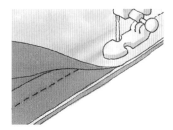

7 When the piping is in place, put the other fabric piece on top, right side down. Pin and stitch the seam through all layers, still with the piping foot or zipper foot on the machine. Avoid stretching either the piping or the fabric as you stitch, otherwise it may pucker. Grade the seam.

8 When piping alongside a zipper opening, it will look better if you pipe the edges of the pieces at the side rather than the edge of the outside back. Make sure that any piping that finishes at the opening will meet exactly; reduce bulk here as explained in step 6.

RUFFLES

A ruffle makes a fun, frivolous alternative to a skirt on a slipcover. There are various ways to make a ruffle.

Single ruffle

If your fabric is quite heavy or bulky, a single ruffle is preferable to the second method, but it can be a little flimsy if the fabric is lightweight.

1 Cut strips of fabric on the straight grain or on the bias (depending on whether you prefer a crisp look or a softer effect), to the desired width of the finished ruffle plus 1¼ in (3cm). Cut enough strips to make the total width, after they are joined, 2–3 times the length of the edge you are stitching it to, depending on how much fullness you want. Generally speaking, the deeper the ruffle, the fuller it should be.

2 Join the ends of the strips into one long strip using plain seams. If the ruffle needs to be stitched into a ring (i.e., if there is no opening), join the ends of the long strip, too. Press the seams open.

3 Press under ¼ in (5mm) and then another ⅜ in (1cm) along the lower edge, and along the ends if they are not joined together. Stitch.

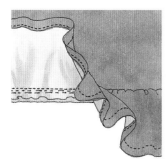

4 To attach the ruffle to the lower edge of the cover, gather it first (see Gathers, page 110). Pin the top edge of the ruffle to the lower edge of the cover with right sides together and raw edges even. If there is an opening, line up the hemmed ends of the ruffle with the finished edge of the opening. Stitch a ⅝ in (1.5cm) seam. Press the seam toward the cover.

Double ruffle

This is neater than a single ruffle but is not suitable for very heavy fabrics.

1 Begin the ruffle as for the single ruffle, steps 1 and 2, but cut the fabric strips to a width equal to twice the desired finished width plus 1¼ in (3cm).

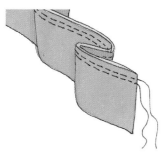

2 If the ruffle is not stitched into a ring, finish the ends by folding the ruffle in half lengthwise, with right sides together, and stitching across the ends. Snip off the corner of the seam allowance, and turn right side out. Press the ends and, with the raw edges even, press the fold along the whole length. Machine baste just inside the ⅝ in (1.5cm) seamline. Attach the ruffle as for a single ruffle, step 4.

Double-edged ruffle

Sometimes known as a butterfly ruffle, this has two finished edges with gathers in between.

1 Make the ruffle as for the single ruffle, steps 1, 2, and 3, but hem the top edge in the same way as the lower edge. Gather the ruffle down the center or off-center.

2 Pin the wrong side of the ruffle to the right side of the cover, and topstitch down the center of the gathers. You can now either remove the gathering threads or conceal them by topstitching ribbon or braid over them.

Piped ruffle

1 To add piping and a ruffle to the lower edge of a cover, machine baste piping to the right side of the lower edge.

2 Make a single ruffle (see page 121) and pin it on top of the piping, with the raw edges even with those of the piping and the cover.

3 With the piping foot or zipper foot on the machine, stitch a ⅝ in (1.5cm) seam. Grade the seam and then press it toward the cover.

TUCKS

These are stitched folds on either the right or the wrong side of the fabric. They extend from edge to edge of a fabric piece. Unlike released tucks (see page 108), they are not used to control fullness but purely as a decorative trim.

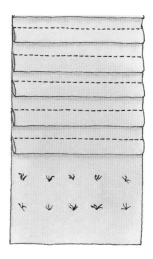

• For plain tucks, mark pairs of stitching lines on the right side with tailor tacks, or on the wrong side with tailor's chalk. The finished tucks will be half as wide as the distance between the two lines in each pair. The tucks should all be the same width, but the spacing between the tucks can be the same or it can gradually increase, as in the variation on page 44—or there can be no extra spacing at all between them. Stitch the pairs of lines together from either the right or the wrong side, stitching always in the same direction. Press the tucks lightly, all in the same direction (using a press cloth if you are pressing from the right side).

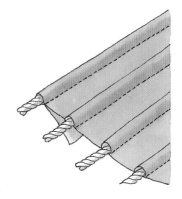

• For corded tucks, make plain tucks (see above), but insert narrow cording inside the fold, and stitch using a piping foot or zipper foot.

BUTTON TUFTING

Button tufting is a good way to add interest to a seat cushion, creating an effect similar to buttoned upholstery. Note that the cover cannot be removed for laundering afterward.

1 You will need covered flat buttons with shanks. Mark the placement of the buttons with large-headed pins in a regular pattern. Cut two 18 in (45cm) strands of strong thread such as buttonhole twist.

2 Take the strands through the shank of the first button, and tie them to the shank halfway along the thread with a double knot.

3 Thread a long upholstery needle with both strands, and push the needle through the cushion from front to back at one of the marked points.

4 At the back of the cushion, remove the needle and tie the shank of a second button with a single knot of the threads. Pull the threads tight until the buttons have created indentations in the cushion. Wrap the threads around the button shank a few times, and then tie a double knot and trim off the ends of the threads.

QUILTING

Because quilting is a decorative way of holding batting in place between layers of fabric, it is ideal for seat covers, which benefit from a little padding.

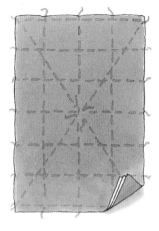

1 Sandwich the batting between the top and bottom of the seat cover, or the cover and its lining. Both pieces of fabric should be right side out. Hand baste the layers together at regular intervals, starting at the center and working outward, first to the corners and then to the sides.

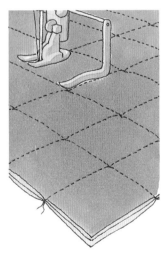

2 Work out a simple quilting pattern that will suit the fabric. It could be squares, diamonds, a tile effect, or lines actually following the fabric pattern. Topstitch through all layers, using a quilting guide-bar attachment or the guide-bar on the walking foot if your machine has either, to keep the stitching straight. Strips of tape stuck on the fabric or hand basting could also be used as guides.

APPLIQUÉ

This technique is not usually associated with slipcovers but in fact can offer an excellent way to decorate them. For example, a stylized star or flower shape in a contrasting fabric that matches piping or a border on the lower edge could be appliquéd to the back of each dining chair in a set. Slipcovers for children's chairs are also prime candidates for appliqué motifs. (Bear in mind, however, that it's much easier to appliqué a motif to a fabric piece than to a completed cover, particularly if you are machine appliquéing it.) Hand appliqué is not as suitable for large motifs as machine appliqué using fusible web, but can be used on smaller motifs.

● To hand appliqué a motif, cut it out from fabric, adding a ¼ in (5mm) seam allowance all around. Pin the center of the motif in place on the fabric piece. Clip into the seam allowance on curves and inward corners. Finger press the seam allowance under the motif as you slipstitch all around the turned-under edge.

● To machine appliqué a motif, cut it out from fabric without adding a seam allowance. Draw the reverse shape on the backing paper of some fusible web, and cut it out, making it very slightly smaller than the motif. Following the manufacturer's instructions, iron the fusible web to the wrong side of the motif. Remove the backing paper and iron the motif to the fabric piece. Zigzag or machine satin stitch around the raw edge.

ADAPTING PROJECTS

The projects in this book cover the main styles of slipcovers, but it is quite likely that the covers you want to make, or the pieces of furniture you want to cover, are different in some way. That shouldn't be a problem—with slipcovers, the designs for arms, legs, skirts, and detailing can all be freely interchanged.

The sections and seams of a slipcover usually correspond roughly to those of the original upholstery, but they don't necessarily have to exactly. You could, for example, add a boxing strip to the top of the back or arm where there wasn't one before, or a whimsical skirt to cover ugly legs. The secret of planning a design is to reduce the whole to its constituent parts.

ARMS

Three of the most common arm shapes are the straight arm, club arm, and scroll arm. The top and front of each are traditionally dealt with in a different way.

Straight arm

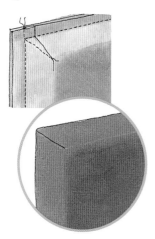

With this arm, the inside arm covers the top and front of the arm as well as the inside. If the angle at the top of the front is fairly sharp, use a dart here. If the angle is more rounded, tiny pleats may work better.

Club arm

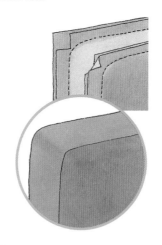

Here, a boxing strip runs along the top and front of the arm, crisply separating the inside arm and outside arm. Clips into the seam allowance at both corners allow the boxing strip to bend 90 degrees.

Scroll arm

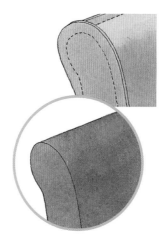

For a chair or sofa with a scroll arm, the inside arm of the slipcover can either curve right over the top of the chair or sofa arm to beneath the scroll on the outside, or stop at the widest part of the scroll. The front arm is usually a separate piece on slipcovers for this style, but sometimes the slipcover inside arm is pleated over the front arm instead of there being a separate piece.

SEATS

Notice whether or not the chair or sofa has cushions. The cover is generally made in the same way regardless of the cushions, but on upholstered chairs you cannot simply add cushions or take them away if this is not part of the basic chair design. Nor can you change their basic shape, since T-cushions in armchairs, and their L-shaped equivalent on sofas, are shaped to fit the seat or back. However, you can alter whether they are box cushions, soft-edged box cushions (with no boxing strip at the front), or mock box cushions (a box shape but without boxing strips).

Also notice whether or not the chair seat projects beyond the arms, as this affects the way the cover is constructed. (Compare, for example, the wing chair seats on pages 10 and 18.)

The point at which the seat of the slipcover finishes can vary a lot. If there is a skirt, it may start at the top of the chair seat, or it could start lower down, perhaps at the base of the chair seat. This affects how the slipcover seat is constructed, as it has to curve down over the front in the latter case. If the chair isn't an armchair, the seat piece will in that instance also curve down over the sides, meaning that small pleats or darts will be needed at the front corners. Or, if it is an armchair, clipping into the seam allowances at the front corners may be all that is necessary to allow the seat piece to curve over the front.

BACKS

On some sofas or chairs, there is a boxing strip running along the top between the inside back and outside back, while on others the inside back piece curves up over the top of the back, to meet the outside back. Yet again, the simple expedient of clipping into the seam allowances at the corners allows the latter construction to work.

ABOVE *Designs are always adaptable. This type of cover is made like the seat of the slipcover on pages 30–33, but as though it had two fronts and no back. The lower edge is hemmed and then trimmed with velvet ribbon.*

SKIRTS

Often, slipcovers have no skirt but, instead, a hemmed lower edge finishing somewhere between the bottom of the seat and the floor. There are, however, many styles of skirts, including separate panels at the sides, dust ruffles, knife-pleated or box-pleated skirts, and tailored skirts with bunched gathers or inverted pleats at the corners. As in dress fashions, skirt lengths are richly varied.

VARIATIONS

There are, of course, many other possibilities. Although the design of the furniture will somewhat restrict the slipcover style, many of the foregoing characteristics can be altered. The very nature of pin-fitting gives you infinite flexibility.

You can also borrow elements from a cover design for one type of furniture to use on a different type. Seat pieces intended for chairs can be adapted into covers for footstools; arm sections from scroll-arm sofas can be cut short and hemmed to become protective armcaps; or the skirt from a sofa slipcover can transform a serving table.

Perhaps the most straightforward project adaptation of all is from a chair slipcover to a sofa slipcover, or vice versa. Sofa slipcovers usually require fabric pieces to be joined together (see page 102), and two closures instead of one, but otherwise the procedure is the same.

Study the component parts of each design in this book and devise projects individually tailored to your own furniture.

index

credits

Quarto would like to thank and acknowledge the following for permission to reproduce their pictures:

Abode 18, 40, 101.
Laura Ashley Ltd 98.
Nina Campbell distributed by Osborne & Little 27, 29.
Cover Up with Charm 105.
Copyright © Homes and Gardens/IPC Syndication 45, 71, 73, 74, 76, 84, 103, 109, 115, 117, 125.
Andrew Martin 10, 66, 69.
The Ravi Design Company, Richmond, B.C., Canada (www.ravidesigncompany.com) 78, 90.
Sanderson 14.
Elizabeth Whiting & Associates 7, 22, 30, 33, 34, 37, 42, 44, 48, 56, 59, 60, 62, 70, 81, 86, 89, 93, 96, 106, 121.
Zoffany (www.zoffany.com) 52, 54.

The author would like to thank Fiona Robertson for her patient and
efficient editorial management; Sheila Volpe for her lively, accessible
design; and, especially, Kate Simunek, whose careful attention to detail
has proved that one illustration really is worth a thousand words.